To Julian Black

with all Best Wishes

from.

Duncan MacNeill

The Bible's Hidden Cosmology

THE BIBLE'S
HIDDEN
COSMOLOGY

Gordon Strachan

Floris Books

First published as *Christ and the Cosmos*
in 1985 by Labarum Publications Ltd

This rewritten and updated version published by Floris Books in 2005
© Gordon Strachan, Edinburgh, 2005

British Library CIP Data available

ISBN 0-86315-479-4

Printed in Great Britain
by Cromwell Press, Wilts.

Contents

William and Heather
Encouraging and generous

ACKNOWLEDGMENTS

From the early days of this venture, my students in the Centre for Continuing Education at the University of Edinburgh have provided me with an invaluable forum for sharing my ideas. In particular, I would like to mention George Rankin, Isabel Lennie and Andrew Gilmour. I would also like to pay tribute to those who first launched me on my cosmological quest: Maryel Gardyne, George Fraser and the late Anne Macaulay. Among astrologers, I would like to thank Morelle Smith, Marie Louise Wiseman and Melanie Reinhart. Margaret Cochran did a great job typing the manuscript and Sarah Frost made many helpful corrections to the text. There are many who have helped me financially. They know who they are and I am very grateful to them.

My publisher Christian Maclean must be congratulated for initiating the venture. My editor, Gale Winskill, has been very patient with my alterations, and the rest of the staff at Floris Books have also been a pleasure to work with.

During the ups and downs of the last few months, my family and a number of friends have helped to keep me on an even keel; among my friends I am most grateful to Rev John R. Smith, Rev William Maundsay and Bishop Brian Smith.

From the beginning I have enjoyed the fellowship and friendship of Elspeth my wife. I am indebted to her for her support in encouraging and helping me to update the text. I want to thank her and our son, Christopher, who has been benignly tolerant of me and all my literary endeavours.

Introduction

Twenty years ago I wrote a book entitled *Christ and the Cosmos*. This current book, *The Bible's Hidden Cosmology*, has been brought up to date and revised, taking into account changes in my own thinking and the context in which I am now writing. This development is reflected by new material, which appears throughout the book, but, nevertheless, it seems to me that the message of this book is, if anything, even more important today than it was twenty years ago, and is an enquiry into the links between the Bible and ancient cosmology. By cosmology I mean the way in which biblical writers and their contemporaries viewed the universe and how that view affected their faith in God. Using a surprisingly sophisticated range of symbol, metaphor, analogy and philosophy, the ancient biblical writers presented a coherent model of the cosmos, a model which, despite its antiquity, has, I believe, much to teach us today. Over the centuries, many aspects of it have at best been ignored, at worst, dangerously distorted by historical Christianity. The wisdom behind it has in effect been hidden. Twenty years ago I believed this to be unfortunate; today I believe it is potentially disastrous.

The 1980s, when I wrote *Christ and the Cosmos*, were anxious times, full of fear of impending nuclear holocaust and ecological disaster. Despite the growth of the ecological movement, the majority of Christians believed in Christ as their personal Saviour and head of the Church, but had no concept of him as 'the one through whom all things were made.' There was a gap between an inward-looking, church-centred religion and a creation-centred, cosmic religion, with potentially tragic consequences: the domesticated religion of the churches was generally both too small and private to be interested in the cosmos and too tolerant of the exploitation of nature to be concerned with its conservation.

This was dangerous enough, but added to that, in America there has been a strand of Christianity, which not only tolerates the exploitation of creation but also looks forward to its destruction as a sign of the beginning of the return of Christ. This form of apocalyptic Christianity has become much stronger since then and teaches that the world will end, not with a whimper, but a bang — a bang which should be welcomed because, according to what is known as post-millennialism, it will usher in the one-thousand-year reign of Christ and all the saints, as prophesied in the Book of Revelation. In 1984, *The Observer* magazine described how in Amarillo, Texas, where nuclear missiles were being built, people positively looked forward to a nuclear holocaust as a sign of the coming of what is called 'the Rapture':

> 'The Rapture' is a phenomenon associated with the Second Coming of Christ, which many people in Amarillo believe to be imminent. Christ will appear and summon the faithful to meet him in the air. Many believe that a nuclear holocaust will be a prelude to the Rapture and that the manufacture of nuclear weapons is therefore part of God's plan.[1]

The dangerous extremism of these apocalyptic views should, one might fairly assume, qualify them for being assigned to the waste bin of history, but tragically nothing could be farther from the case. Using an interpretation of biblical cosmology to be found in certain key books of the Bible such as Daniel, St Paul's letters and Revelation — which read the signs of the times as heralds of catastrophe and judgement, this brand of apocalyptic Christianity has spread ominously over the whole of the USA, and has become a powerful political force. It influences people in positions of immense power and responsibility including the current President, George W. Bush, and his associates, who use it to justify war, imperialism and environmental irresponsibility. As early as 1971, for instance, Ronald Reagan, who held these beliefs, quoted Ezekiel and spoke of Gaddafi's coup in Libya as a sign that Armageddon was not far off:

> Everything is falling into place. It can't be long now. Ezekiel says that fire and brimstone will be rained upon the enemies of God's people. That must mean that they'll be destroyed by nuclear weapons.[2]

Reagan was unsophisticated in his use of apocalyptic theology; Bush is more subtle. Nevertheless, one of Reagan's own religious advisors, James Robison publicly supported George W. Bush and prayed with him on national television during the 2000 Presidential campaign.

This particular spiritual mentor showed his true colours by denouncing peace activists because: 'Any teaching of peace prior to Christ's return is heresy ... It's against the Word of God; it's Antichrist.'[3]

In a recent study of apocalyptic religion and American imperialism, called *An Angel Directs the Storm*, theologian Michael Northcott exposes the thinking behind President Bush and the right wing of the Republican party as based not only on a faulty and dangerously literal interpretation of certain passages of scripture, but also on an inflated sense of prophetic calling to save the world. In his inaugural address in 2001, 'George Bush clearly articulated his belief in his own and America's divine calling to lead the world in an apocalyptic struggle between the forces of good and evil.'[4] In the war-obsessed 2004 Presidential campaign, through the influence of the moral majority of neo-conservatives, religion turned out to be *the* main issue of the election and Bush's successful re-election.

Those, like Bush, who espouse apocalyptic Christianity are in no rush either to pursue peace or to preserve the planet. If the world is going to end tomorrow, why bother to be good stewards of creation today? If peace cannot be achieved before Christ's return why bother to withdraw troops from war zones? As far as these people are concerned, Armageddon, that last great battle between good and evil is on its way — the signs of its imminent arrival are all around, from the creation of the Jewish State in 1948 to the destruction of the Twin Towers in 9/11.

The Battle of Armageddon, despite its infamy, is in fact mentioned only once in the Bible and that is in one of the more judgmental and blood-thirsty passages of the Book of Revelation. Revelation is a minefield of complex symbolism and images of the last times which, especially when read in the antiquated Authorised Version appear to predict the end of the world in horrendous detail, with vivid descriptions of great torments and the horsemen of the apocalypse. There is no hope in this worldview — only disaster. It is at this point that I enter the debate with another very different cosmology. It is drawn, like the apocalyptic theology, from the Book of Revelation, and from other more reliable scriptural writing, and has a very different message — one of hope and harmony.

The fundamentalists believe that the world will end soon with the battle of Armageddon, but it is my thesis that, according to the Bible, it is not the world that will end, but a Cosmic Age. An unexpected ally in this thesis is Dan Brown, author of the international best seller, *The Da Vinci Code*. This book is a fascinating mixture of fact and fiction, which has taken the literary world by storm. It is the story of, among other things, the search for the Holy Grail and involves a murderous race by the Roman Catholic Church to prevent controversial evidence about Jesus emerging at a defining moment in history. This defining moment, according to Brown, is the year 2000, and in his novel the year 2000 not only marks the move into a new millennium but also and more importantly marks the transition from one cosmological age to another — the Age of Pisces to the Age of Aquarius. This period of transition is called the 'End of Days.' Although the 'End of Days' may sound like the end of the world, in the context of the book it is made clear that this does not mean the end of the world. As Langdon, the main character, says the idea that the End of Days means the end of the world,

> is a common misconception. Many religions speak of the End of Days. It refers not to the end of the world, but rather the end of our current age, Pisces, which began at the time of Christ's birth, spanned two thousand years and waned with the passing of the millennium. Now that we've passed into the Age of Aquarius, the End of Days has arrived.[5]

It is quite remarkable that in addition to all the more obvious ingredients which have made this book such compelling reading, this unexpected explanation for the specific timing of the murders in the book should refer to two of the most influential interpretations of history of our times, which are not fictional, and which are currently competing with each other for allegiance, especially in the USA: our times as the end of the world or the end of an Age.

The concept of the End of Days is common parlance in certain groups of the Christian Church, particularly amongst fundamentalists. In America, there are reckoned to be between sixty and one hundred million such Christians, many from the Southern States, many of them right wing, and many of whom voted George W. Bush into the White House. They do not believe that the End of Days is merely a transitional phase. They believe that it will last until the world ends. According to these fundamentalists the end may be quite soon. They can see signs to indicate its imminence in the rise of the anti-Christ in the shape of

Islamic terrorists and the Axis of Evil pitched against the armies of Christ, led by the USA, Britain and Israel. Sooner or later, according to their predictions, the opposing armies will meet in Israel on the plains of Megiddo at Armageddon as prophesied in Revelation (16:16). The battle will be bloody, millions of people will die, but the forces of the Lord will triumph gloriously and usher in the millennium, the thousand-year reign of Christ and his saints. (Rev.20:4)

The frightening truth is that these undoubtedly biblical, but highly speculative apocalyptic predictions are understood *literally*, as graphic descriptions of the main events of future global history by many of the conservatives who voted Republican and surround the American President. With that understanding, they cheer him on to wage incessant war against the infidel. Since 9/11 this mindset has already justified wars against Afghanistan and Iraq, the loss of many basic civil liberties, the reduction of federal resources for social services and environmental protection, and the increased stockpiling of weapons of mass destruction.

In the *Da Vinci Code*, Dan Brown has done a great service to all those who are asking about the truth of history. He has done what the churches have failed to do. By declaring that the literal interpretation of the End of Days as the end of the world is a 'common misconception' he has explained to those who believe in the literal interpretation of apocalyptic that *there is an alternative symbolic meaning*. This alternative has been hidden from most Christians by the mainstream churches who have forgotten or denied the cosmological dimension of the gospel since the early centuries of Christianity. This has been so much the case that those who call themselves New Agers have been condemned as heretics or even demon-possessed by the vast majority of fundamentalists.

They have also been marginalised or dismissed as eccentric by many so-called liberal Christians. It is fascinating that at the same time as the mainstream churches are in decline in Europe, esoteric books such as the *Da Vinci Code* and spiritually open new age thinking is on the increase. This is a sign of our times — perhaps a sign of the new age? Let me again quote the *Da Vinci Code*:

> The Piscean ideal believes that man must be told what to do by higher powers because man is incapable of thinking for himself. Hence it has been a time of fervent religion. Now, however, we

are entering the Age of Aquarius — the water bearer whose ideals claim that man will learn the truth and be able to think for himself. The ideological shift is enormous and it is occurring right now.[6]

Passages like this in the *Da Vinci Code* have obviously struck a chord for many millions of people, and in my book I explore some similar themes, using a method of interpretation, which I believe is in tune with our times.

The method of interpretation by which I have been able uncover the main features of this hidden cosmology will be unfamiliar to most readers. It is an ancient method, which in various forms, was taken for granted from the early centuries of Christianity to the rise of the scientific revolution in the seventeenth century. Most modern biblical scholarship uses methods of interpretation derived from the eighteenth and nineteenth century enlightenment. These have led to a greater and greater degree of historical scepticism. In contradistinction to the liberal sceptics and the literal fundamentalists, the method of interpretation, which I use in this study is as symbolic as it is literal, and as metaphorical as it is sceptical. It distinguishes between history, allegory, parable and myth. It is as scientific as it is spiritual. It is not arbitrary but is based on a symbolic system, which has been integral to the development of Western spiritual education since earliest times. In its most definitive form it derived from Plato and Pythagoras, who themselves are reputed to have propounded it as a result of their travels to ancient Egypt, Mount Carmel and Babylon. Much of the Bible is permeated with insights from this method of interpretation. In the Middle Ages it was known as the Quadrivium, which together with the Trivium, formed the Seven Liberal Arts. It formed the basic mindset of those who were responsible for the flowering of the Gothic Culture from the twelfth to fifteenth centuries, and also those who led the Italian Renaissance in the fifteenth and sixteenth centuries. The fact that since the seventeenth century, with a few notable exceptions, it has been considered outdated does not detract from its profundity, historic importance and cultural and spiritual achievements.

The Trivium consisted of grammar, logic and rhetoric. These were the ancient subjects by which literacy was taught. The Quadrivium consisted of arithmetic, geometry, music and astronomy. These were the four subjects by which numeracy was taught. Numeracy was much more important in general education in the ancient and middle ages than it is today. In modern education the study of number is associated with maths and the mathematical sciences, and is regarded as largely abstract, impersonal and scientific. However, the distinction between science and the humanities was not so sharp in earlier times. This was not only because the sciences were not so highly developed as they are now, but also because during the many centuries in which the tradition of Plato and Pythagoras dominated, number was thought of as literal *and* symbolic. Every number was considered to be a quantity and *also* to have a quality. This applied equally to the Bible. Thus number one, the Monad, was the number one in quantity, but also symbolized God in monotheism because God was One and was the source and origin of all numbers and their symbolism. Two, the dyad was the quantity two, but was also associated with division and strife. Three, the triad, the quantity three, also represented harmony as it was the first number to have a beginning, a middle and an end. Even numbers were considered to be feminine and odd numbers masculine. Thus two plus three making five was considered to be the marriage number because it was the sum of the first feminine and masculine numbers. Geometrically, this was expressed by the pentagon or pentagram. Likewise geometrically one, two, three and four were expressed as a point, a line, a triangle and a square respectively. Six was thought of as the macrocosm because it is a perfect number, since it is the sum of its divisors 1, 2 and 3.

This symbolic attitude to number is no small matter., for numbers are important in most chapters of the Bible. The best-known modern instance in which it is clear that this symbolic understanding has been lost is in the debate between creationism and evolution. Those who take a literal interpretation of the number six insist that, according to the first chapter of Genesis, the world was created in six days and that God rested on the seventh day, the Sabbath. It is on this basis, taking each day as one thousand years, that dispensationalists believe that the biblical date for the beginning of creation is 4004 BC and so we are now entering the seventh millennium which heralds the one-thousand-year reign of Christ. Very few of these Christians realize the symbolic importance of the number six. They have never been taught the long-standing tradition of numerical symbolism expressed by St Augustine and the early Church Fathers, that God had to create the world in six days because six is a mathematically perfect number and he had to conform to his own rules!

> Six is a number perfect in itself and not because God created all
> things in six days; rather the converse is true: God created all
> things in six days because the number is perfect and it would have
> been perfect even if the work of six days did not exist.[7]

This symbolism is by no means outdated or anachronistic because
our divisions of time are still governed by multiples of six hours on a
clock face and sixty seconds in a minute. Thus, for us, the hexagon is
still the symbol of time in the macrocosm for we still set our watches
by it. Likewise, St Augustine saw the beauty of the Trinity in many
created things, which expressed the harmony of threeness. He also saw
the relationship of 1 to 2, the octave, as the harmonious relationship
between the Father and the Son.

For those who know little about the symbolism of the Bible, it will
not be easy to understand that a symbol is always symbolic *of something*. It is never meaningless, arbitrary or fantastic. It always relates to
an ancient tradition where the meaning has been generally accepted. It
is always objective, never subjective. In the Pythagorean and Platonic
Quadrivium, as we have seen, the qualities of numbers as distinct from
their quantities were connected to geometric shapes. They were also
connected to musical ratios, thus 1:1 represented unison, 1:2 the octave,
2:3 the fifth, 3:4 the fourth etc. These ratios were also embodied in
sacred architecture, which in all cultures in the ancient world was modelled on the harmonic resonances of music. The New Jerusalem and the
Temple of Solomon were no exception as we will see.

Thus the first three subjects of the Quadrivium were: arithmetic,
which was the study of numerical quantities and qualities as such;
geometry, which was the study of number in space; and music, which
was the study of number in time. The fourth subject was a combination of the first three applied to the whole cosmos. This was the mathematical study of the stars, astronomy, and their meaning: astrology.
It was thought of as number in space-time. Until the Quadrivium was
separated by modern scientific revolution astronomy and astrology
went together in the same way as every number had a quantity *and* a
quality.

It is popularly thought that astrology is condemned in the Bible but
insofar as this negative assessment is based on texts, there are few and
only found in the Old Testament. In the New Testament, however, it
is a different story. For instance, the three wise men came from the

East asking: 'Where is his star?' The wise men of Christmas time and Epiphany are known as the three kings Melchior, Balthasar and Caspar, but this is a very good example of the way in which the church has successfully hidden the meaning of the story, and has then forgotten the cosmology behind it. Recent translations, such as the New English Bible, the Jerusalem Bible and the New International version, have done much to re-instate the original meaning by translating the wise men as 'Astrologers' which is a more accurate rendering of the Greek word *magoi*.

The best example of the importance of the Seven Liberal Arts in Western spiritual culture can be seen in the famous Western portals of Chartres Cathedral built and carved in the twelfth century. Over the southern door, the one through which visitors enter, are depicted the great men who best symbolize the Trivium and the Quadrivium together with their muses. From the bottom left they are Aristotle as dialectic, Cicero as rhetoric, Euclid as geometry, Boethius as arithmetic, Ptolomy

Fig.I.1. The Seven Liberal Arts in the Western portals of Chartres Cathedral.

as astronomy, Priscian as grammar and Pythagoras as music. In the centre of this arch is the Virgin Mary, symbolizing Sophia, the goddess of Wisdom, who in the Old Testament is *Chokmah*. On her knee is the infant Christ, symbolizing the Logos, the Word made flesh. These represented the Wisdom and Word from whom all these subjects derived.

It might at first appear that to choose the iconography of Chartres Cathedral as the best example of the Quadrivium is highly anachronistic, but this is very much not the case. Every year thousands of people of many religions and none make voluntary pilgrimages to cathedrals across Europe. This is so much the case that it is commonly accepted in ecclesiastical circles that while in Europe attendance at many parish churches is falling, this is not the case with Cathedrals. Cathedrals seem to be as relevant to the spiritual and cultural health of the modern world as they were in medieval times. Nowhere is this more true than at Chartres Cathedral. People flock to Chartres in their thousands because it is a sacred site where they find spiritual refreshment and cultural inspiration. The labyrinth at Chartres is immensely popular and has been reproduced across the world as a tool for meditation and reflection. Chartres is based on the principles of symbolic number, sacred geometry, harmonic theory and cosmic orientation and this is what, unbeknown to them, makes it special for people as they enter. These principles are as valid and relevant as ever and never more so than when applied to the Bible. I believe that a rediscovery of the cosmic dimension of Christianity will help us find a genuine hope for the future, which will replace our pessimistic forebodings with real optimism. It will help us to realize that it is not the *world*, which is about to end, as so many believe, but the *age*. This enquiry I believe, will inspire confidence by helping us to see the horrendous signs of our times as the death throes of one cosmic age and the birth-pangs of another. This is what this book is about.

1. The New Jerusalem and the Cosmos

More than any other book of the Bible, the Revelation of St John has been the seed-bed for apocalyptic ideas. This is perhaps not surprising because the Greek word for revelation is *apocalypse!* The book records a visionary experience, yet it is couched in such vivid symbolic language that it has been taken as imminent historical fact by many Christians down the centuries. Of all its prophetic predictions, the ones which have had the most impact are those regarding the victory of God's army at the battle of Armageddon, the thousand-year reign of the saints with Christ, and the setting up of a holy kingdom centred on the New Jerusalem.

Since the second century when Montanus predicted the Second Coming and the setting up of the New Jerusalem on Phrygian soil, this has been a recurrent theme throughout Christian history, as demonstrated definitively by Norman Cohn in *The Pursuit of the Millennium*. He shows how, particularly in the Middle Ages in movements such as the Brethren of the Free Spirit and among the followers of Thomas Müntzer, John of Leydon and the peasants of the Crusades, the imagery of the New Jerusalem has played a crucial role in the ideology of millennial expectation.[1]

Recently Adrian Gilbert in *The New Jerusalem* has shown convincingly that the Kabbalistic Tree of Life and other esoteric concepts lay behind the replanning and rebuilding of the City of London after the Great Fire of 1666 in the thinking of such leading figures as John Evelyn, Robert Hooke and Sir Christopher Wren. Of the latter he writes: 'In rebuilding London he was putting into practice the hermetic dictum of "as above, so below" and quite literally building a New Jerusalem.'[2] He also draws remarkable parallels between the alignment, plan and astronomy of St Paul's Cathedral and the Church of the Holy Sepulchre, the Dome of the Rock and the Great Pyramid. In so doing he builds on the work of John Michell's pioneering book *The City of Revelation*.

In his book John Michell analyses the geometry and measurements of St John's New Jerusalem, and compares them to those of the Great Pyramid and Stonehenge with startling results.[3] I must acknowledge that, like Adrian Gilbert, I have been very influenced by John Michell's work, although I found the mathematical calculations very hard! However, what I did learn was simple; namely, that in the scriptural text, the Holy City was cubic in shape. Simple though this realization was, it was difficult to understand. How could a city be in the form of a cube? Did Montanus, Thomas Müntzer or Sir Christopher Wren realize that? Do those who today espouse the Armageddon theology know it? If they do, does it make any difference? In attempting to answer this apparently obscure question I was led to uncover the elements of an ancient cosmology, which lies hidden in the Bible. I discovered that such has been the Christian emphasis on what has been called 'Fall-redemption theology' and neglect of 'creation theology' that the true biblical cosmology is nowhere more hidden than in the symbolism of the New Jerusalem.

The cosmic cube

The shape of the New Jerusalem is a perfect cube, for St John says: 'The city lies foursquare ... its length and breadth and height are equal' (Rev.21:16). It could perhaps have been a pyramid, thus offering a convenient downflow for the river of life, as one ingenious scholar suggests,[4] but this is unlikely because pyramids were never associated with the Jews, always with the Egyptians.[5] How could a city be in the shape of a cube, especially one 1,500 miles, 'twelve thousand stadia' (Rev.21:16), in length, breadth and height? It would be some city!

Most commentators solve this riddle by agreeing that both the shape and size of the city should be regarded as symbolic. Some go on to claim that this is St John's version of then current Jewish ideas about the vast cubic city 'exalted on high up to the darkening clouds,'[6] which God would raise up out of the ashes of the Roman destruction of Jerusalem in AD 70.[7] But such speculations raise the question as to whether the New Jerusalem is meant to be understood, even symbolically, as a city in the usual sense of the word. Its extraordinary shape and size might lead us to wonder whether the word *polis*, city, may not be used here to mean something rather different. Reading Lewis Mumford's classic, *The City in History*, I came across just such another meaning which seemed to fit St John's possible intention much better. This was the earliest understanding of *polis* which, according to Mumford, was conceived of as a model of the whole cosmos:

> Beginning as a representation of the cosmos, a means of bringing
> heaven down to earth, the city became a symbol of the possible.
> Utopia was an integral part of its original constitution.[8]

This picture of the city as a 'representation of the cosmos' is very
like St John's vision, for he says on two occasions that he saw the holy
city 'coming down out of heaven from God' (Rev.21:2,10), in much
the same way as Mumford speaks of the original ideal of the city being
conceived of as 'a means of bringing heaven down to earth.' Elsewhere
Mumford elaborates on this interpretation, this time calling the city a
'man-made replica of the universe' which 'opened an attractive vista:
indeed a glimpse of heaven itself.' He then goes on to describe the
ideal life of this cosmic city 'within sight of the Gods and their king,'[9]
in remarkably similar terms to St John's visionary voice: 'Behold,
the dwelling of God is with men. He will dwell with them, and they
shall be his people; and God himself will be with them' (Rev.21:3f). I
believe that it is highly likely that St John did mean the New Jerusalem
to be understood as a representation of the cosmos as much as of the
Church and as a replica of the universe as much as the future home of
the elect.

This cosmic interpretation would certainly explain in what way the
cube was meant to be symbolic — a question which has continually
foxed scholars. Most of them agree that it is a symbol of perfection[10]
and some go on to say that it symbolized perfect symmetry but, to
my knowledge, only M. Newbolt, in *The Book of Unveiling*, offers an
explanation as to why this should be so.[11] He links the cube with the
geometric and numerical philosophy associated with Pythagoras:

> To the Greeks (and St John lived in a Hellenized world) geometry
> had a fascination; to Pythagoras, an Asiatic Greek, number was
> identical with all that is orderly, proper, right, good and beautiful.
> Its clearness and certainty demonstrated the power of reason over
> the formless and unpredictable world of the senses.[12]

Pythagoras was, of course, not merely 'an Asiatic Greek' with a
peculiar penchant for numbers. He was one of the greatest thinkers
of the ancient world and is widely regarded as the founding father of
Western philosophy and science. Yet, as recent scholarship has shown,
he was only the mouthpiece for a cosmology of number and geometry,

which was prevalent throughout the whole of the Middle East many centuries before he lived. Otto Neugebauer, in *The Exact Sciences in Antiquity*, shows that in the third millennium BC the Babylonians knew all about 'reciprocals, multiplications, squares and square roots, cubes and cube roots, the sums of squares and cubes, ... exponential functions, coefficients giving numbers for practical computation ... and numerous metrological calculations giving the area of rectangles, circles,' etc. The famous theorem of Pythagoras was known in Babylon 'more than a thousand years before Pythagoras.'[13] Therefore, I believe Newbolt to be right in suggesting the connection between the cube and Pythagoreanism.

The most famous and influential disciple of Pythagoras was Plato. In the *Timaeus*, he links the four elements, out of which the ancients believed the whole world to be constructed, to four regular geometric solids.[14] These were the tetrahedron, which represented the element of fire; the octahedron, which represented air; the icosahedron, which represented water; and the cube, which represented earth.

> Let us assign the cube to earth; for it is the most immobile of the four bodies and the most retentive of shape, and these are characteristics that must belong to the figure with the most stable faces.[15]

Here we appear to have a problem because if St John was following the Platonic tradition, his cube should only have symbolized the earth and not the cosmos. If he had been a true Platonist his cosmos would have to have been represented by Plato's 'fifth construction, which the god used for embroidering the constellations on the whole heaven.'[16] This fifth regular geometric solid, which represented the cosmos, is usually taken to have been the twelve-faced dodecahedron.

The answer to this apparent discrepancy lies in the fact that Plato did not state explicitly that the dodecahedron was the representation of the cosmos. It was only the four regular solids that he did specify as being used in practical cosmology. The cube, therefore, came to represent the cosmos as well as the earth, because the other three solids were traditionally constructed geometrically within it. Thus the cube of earth, containing all the other elements of the created universe — fire, air and water — was held to contain the cosmos. A variation of this can be seen as late as the seventeenth century in Kepler's model of the solar system.

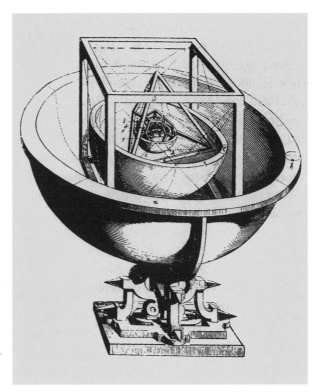

Fig.1.1. Kepler's model of a solar system.

We may say, therefore, that it was most likely that St John was influenced by this tradition and, lest we should worry that we might have to accept him as a crypto-Platonist on that account, let me stress that the geometric cosmology, which Plato got from Pythagoras, can be found in temples, ziggurats and pyramids throughout the ancient world.[17] St John was using the symbolism not so much of 'an Asiatic Greek' as of an apparently universal cosmology, which predated the earliest Greek philosophers by at least a thousand years.

This tradition of a cubic universe is only implicit in the Bible but does surface explicitly in the third century AD Jewish mystical document *The Book of Creation*, the *Sefer Yesira*. In a recent translation, the cosmos is specifically likened to a cube:

> Twelve edges of a cube, divided into six faces, separated in each direction ... And they expand continually for ever and ever, and they are the arms of the universe.[18]

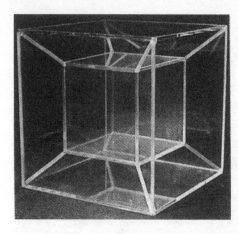

*Fig.1.2. Sagan's model
of a tesseract.*

This is a powerful piece of evidence in confirmation of the cosmic significance of the cubic shape of the New Jerusalem. It also has a strangely modern ring to it for it almost seems to look like an earlier version of the contemporary astronomical theory of the expanding universe, which has been so much in the news in recent years. Carl Sagan, in *Cosmos*, notes the similarity between certain aspects of Hindu cosmology and the 'Steady State' theory, but fails to notice just as startling a similarity between this expanding cubic universe of ancient Jewish mysticism and the so-called 'Big Bang' theory. Had he done so he would have drawn our attention to the peculiar likeness of these two theories when he was endeavouring to explain the mysteries of the fourth dimension by means of a tesseract or hypercube. Although he said he could not show us a tesseract because we are trapped in three-dimensional space, he said he could show us its shadow in three dimensions: 'It resembles two nested cubes, all the vertices connected by lines.'[19] Then, on the basis of this definition, he goes on to explain the theory of the expanding universe.

If we compare Sagan's model of a tesseract, or hypercube, with that of the New Jerusalem as a transparent cube within a cubic universe, the two are found to be identical, for both are nested cubes. The holy city as a paradigm of the cosmos may yet find some friends among modern astrophysicists!

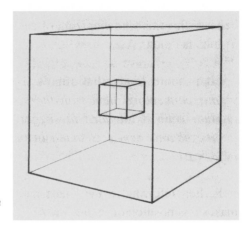

*Fig.1.3. New Jerusalem
as a transparent tube.*

The foundation jewels as the signs of the zodiac

If we turn from the shape to the foundations of the New Jerusalem,
an equally universal symbol can be seen. St John tells us that 'The
foundations of the city were adorned with every jewel' (Rev.21:19),
and these jewels are listed in full. Scholars have often wondered why
all the individual names of the jewels were given and have generally
concluded that they are symbolic of the twelve signs of the zodiac.[20]
But following R.H. Charles' interpretation of Athanasius Kircher,[21]
they have been anxious to point out that the list of constellations is
given in 'exactly the reverse order of the actual path of the sun through
the signs,'[22] and this they attribute to St John's 'polemical motive.'[23] In
the Temple of Solomon, in spite of admitting an obvious link between
the jewels and the stones in the High Priest's breastplate, and that
these stones were taken by both Philo and Josephus as symbolic of
the zodiac, scholars still contend with Charles that 'this order is delib-
erately adopted by John and is intended as a repudiation of the pagan
association of the zodiac.'[24]

Such has been the traditional Christian taboo against astrology
that few writers have dared to question this position. Among those
who have, G.R. Beasley-Murray stands out as particularly coura-
geous. Commenting on the pervasive view that St John is 'not giving
a Christianized version of the "city of the gods" of pagan speculation,'
he says: 'This is doubtful, for the connection is too striking for a rejection to be communicated in this way.'[25] He then goes on to say that he

believes that this Christianizing of pagan speculation is precisely what St John is doing:

> It is more likely that John's listing of the jewel signs *plus his connecting them with the people of God and apostles of the Lamb is intended to suggest that the reality after which the pagans aspire is found in the revelation of God in Jesus Christ.*[26]

Earlier, referring to the shape and size of the New Jerusalem he makes this position even clearer:

> John unhesitatingly appropriated for the city of God ideas relating to the city of the stars which were beloved by the pagan astrologers of his day ... John declares that the reality which corresponds to their imperfect vision is to be found in the city of God and of the Lamb.[27]

I confess that I find this interpretation much more convincing than that of Charles and his followers. I agree with Beasley-Murray that the connection between the jewels and the zodiac is 'too striking for a rejection to be communicated in this way.' I believe that St John was painting a picture of a Christ who was not just head of the Church but who was also the Lord of the farthest bounds of the universe. Scholars have been too quick to deny this astrological dimension; in so doing they have also tended to deny Christ's lordship over his creation. St John's symbolism shows the Lamb on his throne in the midst of his created universe. I believe that Austin Farrar is also correct when he boldly states that the New Jerusalem 'is a four-square city embracing the whole zodiac.'[28]

Further unprejudiced research along these lines confirms this positive link between astrology and the early Judeo-Christian tradition. For instance, J. Massyngberde Ford has no difficulty in proving it archaeologically:

> The signs of the zodiac are depicted in mosaics in synagogues in Palestine, indicating the Jews felt no incongruity in adopting these pagan signs and linking them with Jewish ideas.[29]

Zodiac	Kircher-Charles & Co	Cooper	St John
Aries	amethyst	diamond	jasper (diamond: JB)
Taurus	jacinth	sapphire	sapphire
Gemini	chrysoprase	agate	agate
Cancer	topaz	emerald	emerald
Leo	beryl	sardonyx	sardonyx
Virgo	chrysolite	cornelian	cornelian
Libra	carnelian	opal and lapis lazuli	chrysolite
Scorpio	sardonyx	beryl	beryl
Sagittarius	emerald	topaz	topaz
Capricorn	chalcedony	jet and black onyx	chrysoprase
Aquarius	sapphire	zircon	jacinth (a type of zircon)
Pisces	jasper	amethyst	amethyst

More evidence that the Kircher-Charles hegemony may not stand up much longer to certain areas of scholarship comes from J.C. Cooper's *An Illustrated Encyclopaedia of Traditional Symbols*, where in her entry under 'zodiac' she lists the jewels which in her view correspond to each of the signs.[30] It is extraordinary to note that her list is almost the exact *opposite* of Kircher, Charles and company. The fact that she does not connect her list in any way with the New Jerusalem makes it all the more remarkable. We might parody Charles' famous comment and say: 'This cannot be an accident.' In all except chrysolite and chrysoprase, Cooper's list is exactly the same as St John's — with no reverse order.

Enough has now been said to show that much traditional Christian scholarship has been at pains to deny the cosmic significance of the New Jerusalem and by implication also to deny the cosmic rule of the Lamb on his throne. This tradition must now be regarded as biased and detrimental to the cause of the one in whom 'all things hold together' (Col.1:17).

The gates as the portals of the moon

Moving on now from the foundations to the gates of the city, we encounter the same anti-cosmic prejudice in most commentators who see the pearls — 'the twelve gates were twelve pearls' (Rev.21:21) — as a reference to the pearl of great price (Matt.3:46). Alternatively, influenced once again by Charles,[31] they assert that St John is following a rabbinic tradition that God would one day bring 'pearls thirty cubits long by thirty cubits broad ... and they shall stand in the gates of Jerusalem.'[32] This is predictable but disappointing, because had Charles been open to a more positive view of the possible link between St John's symbolism and 'ethnic speculations regarding the city of the gods,' he would perhaps have seen a parallel between the twelve gates of the city and the twelve 'portals' or 'gates' of the heavens, through which the sun, moon and stars were believed to rise and set in the sky. These he himself elucidates at length in his own classic commentary on the *Book of Enoch*, telling us in detail where to look for the different kinds of portals:

> [Compare 33–36] for portals of winds and stars. In [72–82] sun, moon and stars pass through the same portals, but in [33–36] the stars' portals are small, while in [72] one of the sun's portals is called 'great.'[33]

Alas, there is no lateral thinking in Charles or his disciples. The only scholar who, to my knowledge, accepts this link is William Barclay, in *The Daily Study Bible*, where he speaks of the 'twelve gates through which the stars went in and out upon their business.'[34] If with Barclay we were to accept this gate-portal connection, then J.C. Cooper's interpretation of pearl symbolism becomes most intriguing. She says that the pearl is pre-eminently a lunar symbol. It represents the moon above all things.[35] Would it be reasonable to suggest that the twelve gates-which-are-pearls might well symbolize the twelve 'portals' of the moon and thus the twelve months of the year? If so, quite apart from representing the 'twelve tribes of the sons of Israel' (Rev.21:12) and possibly the pearl of great price, they might also speak of the lordship of the Lamb over time, in the same way as the jewel-zodiac-foundations speak of his lordship over space.

The street as the Milky Way

This 'portals of the moon' interpretation would also be consistent with Beasley-Murray when he suggests that 'the street of the city' (Rev.21:21) was not some oriental high street but was nothing less than the highway of the stars. He makes the claim that 'the model for the street is none other than the Milky Way.'[36] Barclay once more agrees, saying that 'the Milky Way was its great street.'[37]

Adrian Gilbert has done substantial research on the ancient Egyptian belief that the River Nile symbolized the Milky Way. In *The Orion Mystery* he says:

> It was now looking likely that I had stumbled upon the true nature of the pyramids. The Duat (the starry world of Osiris), which stretched along the 'west bank' of the Milky Way corresponded to — indeed was seen as a mirror image of — that region we now call the Memphite Necropolis. It was, of course, not a necropolis at all in the Greek or Western sense of the word; rather the Elysian Fields, the earthly counterpart of the heavenly abode of the king-gods of Egypt — the Egypt, that is of the Pyramid age.[38]

He also makes out a convincing case in *Signs in the Sky*, that the ancient Israelites similarly regarded the River Jordan. They 'Looked upon the River Jordan as symbolizing the Milky Way in just the same way as the Egyptians viewed their own River Nile.'[39] Thus the interpretation of the street of the New Jerusalem as the galaxy is not as strange or unique as it might seem.

The Eden Centre

We have succeeded in finding a cosmic meaning for the cubic shape, the foundations, gates and street of the holy city. What about its contents? What is actually inside? Scholars speak of its gate-towers and numerous streets; hymn writers from Augustine to Samuel Johnson wax eloquent over its halls, houses, turrets and pinnacles,[40] and artists, from Hans Lufft illustrating Luther's Bible to Annie Vallotton in Today's English Version, show it crammed full of the same urban features (see next page). But where are all these

*Fig.1.4. Hans Lufft's
New Jerusalem.*

splendid civic amenities to be found in the text? Where does St John
speak of streets in the plural (*plateia* is singular)?[41] Where does he
mention gate-*towers* or any towers for that matter? Where does he
describe any halls, houses, turrets or pinnacles? The answer to all
these questions is, of course, that he doesn't make a single reference
to any of them. They simply cannot be found. All of them are inferences from the misconceived notion that by 'city' St John meant a
metropolis. We have seen that the evidence against this urban meaning is considerable, and when we examine what the text *does say* it
becomes overwhelming. St John makes it quite clear that the only
things inside the walls, apart from the street already referred to, are
the throne of God and the Lamb, the river of the water of life, and
the tree of life:

> Then he showed me the river of the water of life, bright as crystal,
> flowing from the throne of God and of the Lamb through the
> middle of the street of the city; also on either side of the river,
> the tree of life with its twelve kinds of fruit, yielding its fruit
> each month; and the leaves of the tree were for the healing of the
> nations. (Rev.22:1f)

Whatever the river and the tree of life were meant to symbolize, one
thing is certain — they were not images of a conurbation. How they
were ever thought to be so is almost inexplicable. Once we change our
preconceptions from an ecclesiastical town to an image of the cosmos,

Fig.1.5. Annie Vallotton's New Jerusalem.

then the meaning of the symbolism becomes obvious. St John's vision was of a 'new heaven *and* a new earth.' (Rev.21:1) So far, all the details we have examined have been found to be symbolic of the heavens. Here at last we have been given symbols of the earth. I fail to see what meaning can be given to the river of the water of life and the tree of life other than that of an earthly rural paradise. They are so reminiscent of the story of the garden of Eden (Gen.2:9f) that I believe they must be taken as the ecological equivalent of all that has been said so far about cosmology. St John is telling us that the Lamb on his throne is also Lord of a new earth order in which harmony will be restored as at the beginning. Thus the Bible not only begins, but also ends with a garden. This is of paramount importance for the Green Movement today as it seeks to *de-school* Western technological man from the false belief that progress consists in abandoning rural roots in favour of larger and larger cities.

Crystal consciousness

Having now completed this cosmic and ecological interpretation of the New Jerusalem, it only remains to offer some explanation for the crystalline nature of the whole structure. St John says that it had 'radiance like a most rare jewel, like a jasper, clear as crystal' (Rev.21:11). He also says: 'The wall was built of jasper, while the city was built of pure gold, clear as glass' (Rev.21:18). All of this suggests that the whole edifice was made of crystal, not just the foundations. This would agree with the basic physics of crystal shapes, of which a prominent one is the cube, as anyone who chooses to examine this branch of science can confirm.[42] Beyond the scientific authenticity of cubic crystals there has in recent years been a resurgence of interest in the powerful psychic and spiritual properties of crystals.

What could be described as a crystal-mysticism has grown up as an aspect of current developments in complementary medicine. Crystal is thought of in these circles as a symbol of the spirit. The 'state of transparency' is reckoned to be the manifestation of the harmonious union of opposites because it is matter, which exists, yet seems not to exist. It is solid, yet also transparent. Mellie Uyldert, in *The Magic of Precious Stones*, has absorbing chapters on the differing powers of gems and their link with astrology, religion and healing.[43] Ra Bonewitz also develops the latter aspect in *Cosmic crystals, crystal consciousness and the New Age*. His chapters on crystal energies and personal and planetary healing through crystals, raise fundamental questions about the links between modern crystallography and ancient mysticism. As a scientist as well as a mystic, Bonewitz believes that reality inhabits neither the material nor the spiritual in its entirety but 'dwells equally in both.'[44] He goes so far as to say that it is this concept of the marriage of matter and spirit which has given birth to this most arresting book. His use of the metaphor of marriage in this connection once again points us back to the holy city which St John describes as being 'prepared as a bride adorned for her husband' (Rev.21:2), and as 'the Bride, the wife of the Lamb' (Rev.21:9). The New Jerusalem as the Bride, the wife of the Lamb, does seem to fit the idea of the union of opposites, matter and spirit, of which Bonewitz and others speak. This is equally the case in his comments about planetary healing for St John says that 'the leaves of the tree were for the healing of the nations' (Rev.22:2).

In *The World Atlas of Mysteries*, Francis Hitching speaks of three Russian scientists in the 1960s who came to believe through their researches, that planet earth was originally, and is still, essentially crystalline. In the chapter 'Crystalline Planet' he summarizes their contention that our world is constructed out of twelve pentagonal slabs which cover the globe and thus make it a dodecahedron.[45] This takes us back to Plato, who said 'the real earth viewed from above is supposed to look like one of those balls made out of twelve pieces of skin sewn together.'[46] Whether or not this Russian theory is true, it is interesting

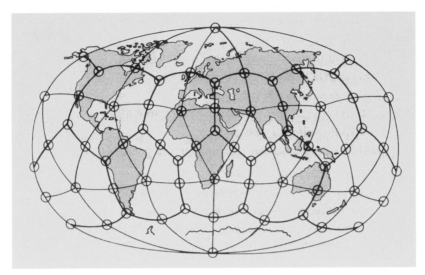

Fig.1.6. Crystalline Planet.

to speculate on the possibility. Was the earth originally a crystalline dodecahedron?

St John is quite clear that the unity of heaven and earth in the crystal of the New Jerusalem symbolizes the mystical marriage between Christ and his creation. Bonewitz reminds us that 'crystal is a perfect expression of the divine mind ... When you tune in to the energy of the crystal, you are tuning in to a very precise aspect of the divine mind.'[47] Whether in the microcosm or the macrocosm it seems crystals can still communicate something of the message that came to St John. It is still a message for healing, not for disease, for harmony not discord, for revelation not apocalypse.

As I read Bonewitz and Hitching I couldn't help remembering Milton's *Ode on the Morning of Christ's Nativity*. It seemed to take on a new meaning:

> Ring out, ye crystal spheres!
> Once bless our human ears,
> If you have power to touch our senses so;
> And let your silver chime
> Move in melodious time;
> And let the base of Heaven's deep organ blow;
> And with your ninefold harmony
> Make up full consort to the angelic symphony.

For if such holy song
Enwrap your fancy long,
Time will run back, and fetch the age of gold;
And speckled vanity
Will sicken soon and die,
And leprous sin will melt from earthly mould;
And Hell itself will pass away,
And leave her dolorous mansions to the peering day.

2. The Sacred Geometry of
the New Jerusalem

To supplement our examination of St John's vision of the New Jerusalem, a geometric figure might be constructed to help in the process of changing the picture of the holy city from a heavenly metropolis to an image of the cosmos, as already described. One picture is worth a thousand words and a change of model can help us see the whole thing in a completely new way.

I propose drawing a model of the New Jerusalem according to the principles of sacred geometry.[1] Sacred geometry, as Robert Lawlor defines it in *Sacred Geometry, Philosophy and Practice*, was the ancient art-science of laying bare in two dimensions the underlying structure of the universe. Only straight-edge and compasses were allowed, and each number, ratio and shape corresponded to a spiritual reality or archetype according to the principle of correspondence which, simply stated, is: 'as above, so below;' or 'as in the macrocosm, so in the microcosm.'[2]

The inner circle

We start with a dot or point representing the One, that is, God as microcosm. Round it we draw a circle representing the All, that is God as macrocosm. As Hermes Trismegistus is reputed to have said: 'God is a circle whose centre is everywhere and circumference is nowhere.'[3]

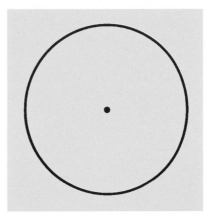

Fig.2.1. The One and the All.

Fig.2.2. (a) The axis-mundi and the rivers of Eden; and Fig.2.2 (b) The Chi-rho.

Keeping our compasses at the same span, we mark off the circumference of the circle into six equal portions, the first mark being at the top or bottom. Then we join these six points to the centre. This figure in its vertical line now represents the *axis mundi* or axle of the world, around which the ancients believed the universe revolved. It also stands for the tree of life in the Garden of Eden and in the New Jerusalem. The diagonal lines which intersect it represent the four rivers of Eden and the river of the water of life in the New Jerusalem. Altogether these six lines symbolize the cross of Christ and the *Chi-Rho*, or *labarum* of the Constantinian Church — that is, the first two letters of Christ's name in Greek.[4]

Now we join up the points of the axes where they touch the circumference, thus making a six-sided hexagon. This hexagon is the same as a cube when seen at an angle of 45 degrees with the foremost point and the rearmost point coinciding in the centre. This cube-as-hexagon is a most important figure and can easily be seen to be a model of the cube of the New Jerusalem. Let us picture Jesus Christ as the central point of the circle where all the lines meet. This is him on his 'throne' with his Father, the one in whom 'all things hold together' (Col.1:17). St John says: 'I saw no temple in the city, for its temple is the Lord God Almighty and the Lamb.' (Rev.21:22) We can see from this simple geometric figure how Christ can be pictured as Saviour, in the cross and in the *Chi-Rho*, and as Creator in the central point

Fig.2.3. (a) The cube as hexagon; and Fig.2.3. (b) The intermediate circles.

which holds all things together. This is most important. Nothing that I say is designed to undermine the gospel of Christ as Saviour, but I do wish to see him as Creator in a way that does equal justice to his twofold function. For unless the Saviour can also be seen as the Creator, we shall remain trapped within the dualism which has separated Christians from creation and contributed so much to our present ecological impasse.

From this figure we can see how Christ as both Creator and Saviour becomes, geometrically, the temple himself. He literally *is* the the temple with his Father-God. This links up with his speaking of 'the temple of his body' (John 2:19). It also links up with all those who are 'in Christ,' for St Paul says: 'Do you not know that you are God's temple?' (1Cor.3:16), and 'Do you not know that your body is a temple of the Holy Spirit?' (1Cor.6:19). We may therefore also take this cube-as-hexagon to represent the Church, not so much as an organization or building but more as a spiritual and physical relationship between Christ and the members of his body. For he is not only the 'first-born of all creation,' he is also the 'head of the body, the church,' as St Paul says:

He is head of the body, the church; he is the beginning, the first-born from the dead, that in everything he might be pre-eminent. For in him all the fullness of God was pleased to dwell, and through him to reconcile to himself all things, whether in earth or in heaven, making peace by the blood of his cross. (Col.1:18–20)

This way of looking at the person and work of Christ has a close affinity with the tradition of mystical thought which sees him as the still point of light at the centre of the turning world. St John says: 'The city has no need of sun or moon to shine upon it, for the glory of God is its light, and its lamp is the Lamb' (Rev.21:23). Jesus said: 'I am the light of the world' (John 8:12). The Nicene Creed calls him 'Light from Light.' T.S. Eliot in *Burnt Norton* is speaking from this biblical and mystical background when he writes:

> At the still point of the turning world. Neither flesh
>   nor fleshless;
> Neither from nor towards at the still point, there
>   the dance is,
> But neither arrest nor movement ...
>   Except for the point, the still point,
> There would be no dance, and there is only the
>   dance.[5]

The intermediate circles

Let us now move on to the next stage in the construction of our model. With compasses still at the length of the radius of the circle, from each of the points where the axes touch the circumference, describe segments of arcs furthest away from the centre of the circle. Then extend each of the axes outwards until they cross these arcs. With these intersection points as the centres, describe six circles round the central circle. You will find that, drawn accurately, these six circles touch the central circle and each other tangentially. (see Fig.2.3. (b), p. 41)

You have now drawn a picture of the beginning of all creation when God created everything in six days and rested on the seventh (Gen.1–2:3). These six circles also symbolize the six days of the working week surrounding the sabbath. Could they perhaps also be 'the seven spirits who are before his throne' (Rev.1:4), or 'the seven angels who had the seven bowls full of the seven last plagues' (Rev.21:9)?

These seven circles also represent the solar system with the Sun at the centre and the Moon, Mars, Mercury, Jupiter, Venus and Saturn round about. These were the seven planets of ancient astronomy which are still associated with the seven days of the week, namely: Sunday = Sun's-day; Monday = Moon's-day; Tuesday = Mars'-day (mardi); Wednesday = Mercury's-day (mercredi, Wodensday); Thursday = Jupiter's-day (jeudi, Thorsday); Friday = Venus'-day (vendredi, Friasday); Saturday = Saturn's-day. For clarity of derivation I have put in the French and Norse equivalents.

If you now join the centres of the six outer circles, you will have formed another cube-as-hexagon, so that the whole figure has become a cube-as-hexagon within a cube-as-hexagon. It has in fact become a hypercube or tesseract, as Carl Sagan described it: 'It resembles two nested cubes, all the vertices connected by lines.' In an extraordinary way we have once again suddenly leapt from what we thought was purely an ancient way of picturing the cosmos, to contemporary astrophysics. If we now allow ourselves to return to the *Sefer Yesira*, the *Book of Creation*, we can see how our model can also be further developed to express the 'Twelve edges of a cube' which 'expand continually for ever and ever.'

The outer circles

The ideas of the expanding universe, the nested cubes of the tesseract, the cube of the cosmos and the New Jerusalem as cosmic model, all come together in this geometric figure and can be even further eluci-dated if we enlarge it yet again. On the same principle as before, extend the six axes until they cross the segments of arcs formed by the circum-ferences of circles whose centres are the points at which these axes cross the outer circumference of the six circles. At these intersections describe six circles all of the same radii as the others. Join the centres of these six outer circles and describe equal circles in the six gaps between them by the same means. You now have a cube-as-hexagon within a cube-as-hexagon within a cube-as-hexagon. These are the microcosm, the intermediate mesocosm and the macrocosm (see next page). The macrocosmic cube represents the universe expanding for ever and ever and the twelve outer circles represent the twelve divisions of the heav-ens, the constellations of the zodiac and the foundations of the New Jerusalem 'adorned with every jewel.' They also symbolize 'the names

Fig.2.4. (a) The mesocosm; and Fig.2.4. (b) The macrocosm.

of the twelve tribes of the sons of Israel' (Rev.21:12) and 'the twelve names of the twelve apostles of the Lamb' (Rev.21:14).

We have now completed the sacred geometry of the New Jerusalem as a 'representation of the cosmos' and a 'replica of the universe.' It offers a simple yet profound picture which may help us to think holistically about Jesus Christ as the one through whom all things were made (John 1:3). It would also appear to unite the container, extensive and geometric concepts of space, which have been at the centre of speculation in theoretical physics for the last three hundred years.

Solomon's Seal

Before we finish this particular exercise I would like to mention one more geometric symbol. If we return to the elements of our paradigm, that is, to the central circle with the six circles round it, and if we remove all traces of the cube-as-hexagon, and then join the centres of the first, third and fifth circles, and the centres of the second, fourth and sixth, we have described two intersecting equilateral triangles. If we then remove the circles, we are left with only these two triangles. This figure is the six-pointed star known as Solomon's Seal, a most important geometric construction, as J.C. Cooper explains:

Fig.2.5. (a) Solomon's Seal; and Fig.2.5. (b) The T'ai Chi.

The double triangle, the six-pointed star, the Seal of Solomon, the Mogun David, indicates that 'every true analogy must be applied universally,' 'as above so below;' it is the union of opposites, male and female, positive and negative; fire and water; evolution and involution; interpenetration, each being the image of the other; the perfect balance of complementary forces ... As the Seal of Solomon it is also the figure of the Preserver and gives spirit power over matter.[6]

In other words it is the biblical equivalent of the Chinese symbol of the yin-yang balance, the *T'ai Chi*.

The *T'ai Chi* or *Ta ki* has become very well-known in recent years because of the influence of Taoist philosophy in the West, particularly through such books as *The Tao of Physics* and *The Turning Point* by Fritjof Capra. Like Solomon's Seal, it symbolizes the union of opposites held together in harmonious balance, interpenetrating and interdependent, each containing the germ of the other in perpetual alternation.

All the meanings of Solomon's Seal listed by Cooper comple-ment, to a remarkable degree, those which we have already drawn out of our own geometric model. It is also extraordinary that, as with the cubic universe and the tesseract, recent advances in elec-tron microscopy reveal how similar the structure of Solomon's Seal is to the basic structure of crystal. Professor Gareth Thomas of the

Fig.2.6. Zone axis pattern of a silicon crystal.

University of California has demonstrated, using convergent beam microscopy, that if a sharply focused beam of electrons, moving at over half the speed of light, is bounced off a silicon crystal, an image is formed (a zone axis pattern) of a complex geometric structure at the heart of which are two equilateral triangles intersecting in the form of Solomon's Seal. At the centre of this is a luminous dot.[7] If we remember to what extent the silicon chip is responsible for our present communications revolution, we shall come nearer to realizing that in sacred geometry and these biblical texts, we are encountering fundamental truths, which are just as relevant today as they ever were. Modern science is stumbling upon this ancient wisdom in spite of its desire to be exclusively materialistic — to be concerned only with knowledge, not wisdom. Perhaps by bringing these two disciplines together, the old and the new, a union of opposites, a 'perfect balance of complementary forces' could be achieved.

But the final question must be: why is Solomon's Seal — or the Star of David as it is popularly called — still the symbol of the Jews? Why is it that this six-pointed star is seen flying on the Israeli national flag? Could one answer be that the link between the Bible and Sacred geometry is very strong — so strong that those who believed in the scriptures saw the geometric symbol of the union of opposites as the perfect expression of their faith? If this is so then we can only lament the extent to which that link has been broken and that wisdom lost.

It is becoming increasingly clear that what we are dealing with in this field is not something which is peripheral to the Bible. It is not eccentric or marginal. It is a lost tradition, which comes as much from the heart of the scriptures as the forgotten truths about the cosmic Christ.

3. The Temple and the Cosmos

The cubic shape of the New Jerusalem is modelled on the Holy of Holies in Solomon's temple, where we are told: 'The inner sanctuary was twenty cubits long, twenty cubits wide and twenty cubits high' (1 Kings 6:20). St John saw the whole city 'as itself the Holy of Holies' vastly magnified.[1] It had all become holy because 'Christ has destroyed the veil of separation which kept men out and has opened a new and living way by which all are invited to approach.'[2]

If we examine the architectural proportions of the temple, as given in the Old Testament, we shall find that, even in the tenth century BC, the same geometric and numerical cosmology is evident as in the New Jerusalem. Nigel Pennick, in his chapter on the Hebrews in Sacred Geometry, explains the ancient belief that the little world or microcosm of the holy buildings was supposed to correspond in every detail to the macrocosm of the universe:

> As a microcosm, it was necessary that the temple or tabernacle should directly reflect in its dimensions, geometry and orientation, the conditions and structure of the macrocosm of which it was at once an image and a means of direct access. Indeed Josephus asserts that 'this proportion of the measures of the Tabernacle [or temple] proved to be an imitation of the system of the world.'[3]

The musical measures of the temple

The question still remains, why was the cosmos imagined to be a cube? We have already answered this in part by saying that it was held to contain the other three platonic solids and the elements which they represented. Pennick however gives another reason which relates the Holy of Holies in the temple directly to the New Jerusalem: 'the symbolic cube ... like the City of Revelation or the Jewish Holy of Holies, contains the consonances of the Universe.'[4] Here Pennick is referring to yet another important dimension of the ancient wisdom, namely the link between architectural proportion and the ratios of musical notes. For the ancient world — not just Pythagoras — all things were

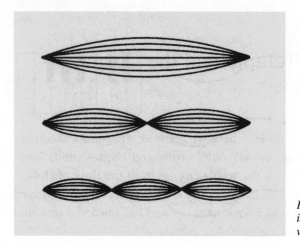

Fig.3.1. The musical intervals of string vibrations.

numbers and all numbers had correspondences in every area of knowledge. The cube was symbolic of all the consonances in music because the ratios of all its sides are 1:1. The ratio of 1:1 in music represents the note of unison or the full string-length, and the full string-length contains within itself the vibrations of all the other musical intervals. These notes within the full string-length are known as 'overtones,' as Percy Scholes describes:

> The string simultaneously vibrates as a whole and also in two and three equal parts, respectively (and also of course, in other smaller parts). Its vibration as a whole produces the fundamental note; in halves the note an octave higher; and in thirds the note a twelfth higher — and so on with the smaller simultaneous divisions not shown here.[5]

The cube was the architectural equivalent of the full string-length — the fundamental — and was thus held to contain the whole of the overtone series, i.e. all the consonances of the universe. Guy Murchie, in *Music of the Spheres*, adds yet another harmonic analogy to the sacredness of the cube in ancient cosmology. This was to do with the ratio of its faces and edges to its points: 'Even the abstract cube was held sacred because its eight corners form the harmonic mean between its six faces and its twelve edges.'[6] In other words, if twelve is the fundamental and six the octave, then eight is the dominant fifth.

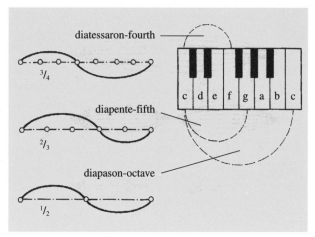

Fig.3.2. The ratios of musical intervals.

   This musical interpretation of the proportions of the Holy of Holies applied equally to the other larger but less sacred chamber of the temple, the Holy Place, as can be demonstrated by analyzing its proportions along the same lines. We are told that the overall size of these two adjacent chambers was 'sixty cubits long, twenty cubits wide and thirty cubits high' (1Kings 6:2). This building was then partitioned off at twenty cubits to make the inner sanctuary, the Holy of Holies. So 'the nave in front of the inner sanctuary was forty cubits long' (1Kings 6:17). Thus the proportions of the Holy Place were 40 × 30 × 20 cubits. If these are divided by their highest common factor, 10, they become 4 × 3 × 2. If these are then put into three sets of ratios, they become 1 to 2 (the same as 2 to 4), 2 to 3, and 3 to 4. As fractions, these ratios are $^1/_2$, $^2/_3$, $^3/_4$. It is an extraordinary fact that these ratios and fractions are exactly the same as those which mark the musical intervals of the octave, the fifth and the fourth or, as the Greeks later called them, the diapason, the diapente and the diatessaron.[7]

   The Holy Place can therefore be said to have expressed, in ratios of architectural proportion, the same musical tones, which were implicit in the unison or fundamental note of the Holy of Holies.

   These four notes — the fundamental, the octave, the fifth and the fourth — are known as the *perfect* consonances because they are invariable. They cannot be changed into the major or minor key and are therefore the very basis of harmony. The other consonances of the scale — the third and the sixth — are thought of as *imperfect* because they are variable. However, both of these were also built into the

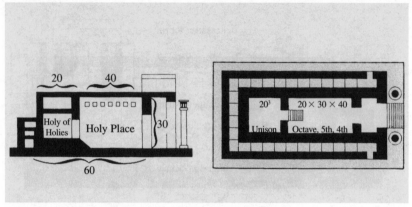

Fig.3.3. Temple measurements and proportions.

construction of the temple because the 40 × 30 cubit rectangles, which formed the two longer sides of the Holy Place, were thought of as two 3:4:5 triangles sharing the same hypotenuse.

The 3:4:5 triangle was held to correspond to these two imperfect consonances as well as the fourth because, if the full string-length is taken as corresponding to the hypotenuse of 5 units, then the ratios it forms with the other two sides are 4 to 5 and 3 to 5, and these correspond to the intervals of the major third and the sixth.

Although there are no explicit biblical references to this musical interpretation of the temple proportions, there are many clues to it implicit in the important role which the Israelites attributed to music in the temple tradition, beginning with King David, 'the sweet psalmist of Israel' (2Sam.23:1) who, according to the Chronicler, received the measurements 'from the hand of the Lord' (1Chr.28:11–19). It is particularly intriguing to note in this connection that, in the Chronicler's version of the dedication of the temple, it was when the 288 levitical

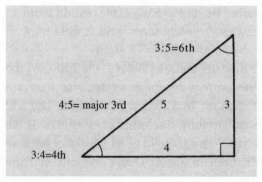

Fig.3.4. The musical ratios of the 3, 4, 5 triangle.

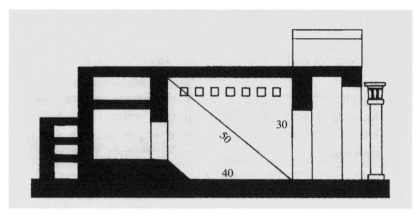

Fig.3.5. The 3, 4, 5 triangles in the Holy Place.

singers (1Chr.25:7) and the 'hundred and twenty priests who were trumpeters ... raised the song' to God 'in unison,' that 'the house of the Lord, was filled with a cloud' and 'the glory of the Lord filled the house of God.' (2Chr.5:12–14) This is usually taken to be a reference to the cloud which covered Mount Sinai, when God revealed his glory and his law to Moses (Exod.24:15–18). The implication is that Solomon and his people, having obediently built everything 'according to the plan,' had now found divine approbation. The inner connection between Mount Sinai and the temple was that the latter had been built as a permanent home for the Ark of the Covenant, the box, which contained the very tablets of stone on which Moses had originally written the law. But we can now also legitimately interpret this story according to our musical cosmology, for it would fit all that we have discovered about the temple measurements and their correspondence to the consonances of the universe. According to this, the Chronicler would be telling us that the laws of harmony were seen as an expression of the Torah and that the temple, as the architectural embodiment of that harmony, as 'frozen music,'[8] rang true. The singers and trumpeters chimed perfectly with the harmoniously proportioned building. As they raised their song 'in unison,' all the consonances in this perfect microcosm would have begun to vibrate. By his own law of correspondence God was bound to answer from the macrocosm.

It is extraordinary how this ancient theory of cosmic resonance and of sacred architecture as frozen music is in agreement with recent developments in theoretical physics. In so-called 'String Theory' it would appear that modern notions echo ancient ones and that what we in the West might call Pythagorean ideas have today become new again. In *The Elegant Universe*, Brian Greene explains the belief that all matter is made up of millions of tiny strings, vibrating like a violin:

> To understand this, let's first think about more familiar strings, such as those on a violin. Each string can undergo a huge variety (in fact, infinite in number) of different vibrational patterns known as resonances, such as those shown in figure 6.1 [see Fig.3.6. below]. These are the wave patterns whose peaks and troughs are evenly spaced and fit perfectly between the string's two fixed endpoints. Our ears sense these different resonant vibrational patterns as different musical notes. The strings in string theory have similar properties. There are resonant vibrational patterns that the string can support by virtue of their evenly spaced peaks and troughs exactly fitting along its special extent. Some examples are given in Figure 6.2 [see Fig.3.6. below]. Here's the central fact: Just as the different vibrational patterns of a violin string give rise to different musical notes, the different vibrational patterns of a fundamental string gives rise to different masses and force

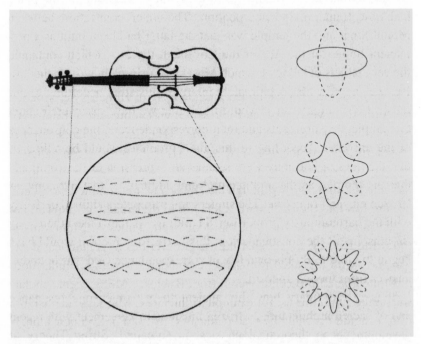

Fig.3.6. Strings on a violin vibrating in resonance. Similarly loops in string theory can vibrate in resonance patterns.

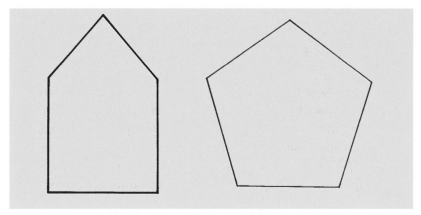

Fig.3.7. (a) Burney's arched door; and Fig.3.7. (b) The pentagonal door.

changes. As this is the crucial point, let's say it again. According to string theory, the properties of an elementary 'particle' — its mass and various force changes — are determined by the precise resonant pattern of vibration that its internal string executes.[9]

Having examined the musical measurements of the Holy of Holies and the Holy Place, I would now like to take a close look at the door which connected these two rooms.

The pentagonal door

The shape of the door which led into the Holy of Holies is described in the Authorized Version of the Bible as if it was in breadth, a fifth part of the total part of the chamber, for it says: 'The lintel and the side posts were a fifth part of the wall' (1Kings 6:31). C.F. Burney, contradicting many earlier scholars who had accepted this, says that this translation is 'alien to the context.'[10] Although the Hebrew text is admittedly obscure, he suggests that the 'fifth part' refers not to the breadth of the wall but to the jambs or side posts of the door itself. James A. Montgomery, following Burney, agrees that the verse describes a 'pentagonal door-way, i.e., with a peaked roof' and he compares it with a similar door illustrated on a third century coin from Byblos.[11] More recent scholar-ship agrees with this as, for example, John Gray, who says 'hamisit ("a fifth") should probably be read hamusot ("fivefold") i.e. a pentagon.'[12]

This scholarly consensus has been reflected in many more recent translations of the Bible. For instance, the Revised Standard Version

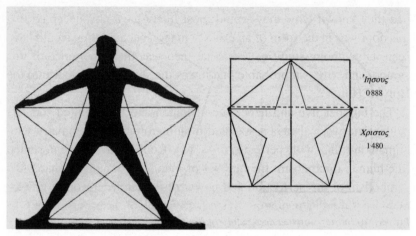

Fig.3.8. (a) Man as the pentagon; and Fig.3.8. (b) Side of a pentagon.

of the Bible says: 'The lintel and the door posts were pentagonal,' the
Living Bible, that the doorway was 'a five-sided opening,' and the New
International Version that the doors had 'five-sided jambs.'

But there still remains an uncertainty as to what exactly the pentagonal door would have looked like. Burney gives a small illustration
of a normal door with an angular arch. Other scholars would probably agree with him, and with Montgomery who describes the door
as having a 'peaked roof.' This may very well have been the case and,
with the Hebrew text being corrupt, no one will ever know for certain.
Nevertheless, in the light of all that has been said so far about the
sacred geometry built into Solomon's temple, it would be reasonable
to suggest that this door might actually have been built in the shape of
an exact pentagon.

I put this suggestion forward because the pentagon was thought of
as one of the most powerful of geometric symbols and therefore would
have been a most appropriate shape for such a uniquely important
doorway. It would also be consistent with the sacred geometry of the
whole building as already described. None of the commentators cited
mentions this as a possibility, but then only one of them commenting
earlier on the Holy of Holies (1Kings 6:20) makes even the briefest
reference to the fact that it was a cube.[13] Although this is disappointing,
it is not surprising because, as we have noted with regard to the New
Jerusalem, geometric considerations have been largely neglected by
biblical scholars. I make this point to emphasize that, had commentators regarded the cubic shape of the Holy of Holies as important and

had they known why, they would most likely have also accepted that this door was in the form of an exact pentagon because they would have seen its symbolic significance. What then was the importance of this symbol and why is it probable that it was the shape of the door into the Holy of Holies?

The number five and hence the pentagon and five-pointed star, the pentagram, were always associated in numerology and geometry with humankind and with perfection. As J.C. Cooper says, it represented 'the human microcosm; the number of man. The pentagon, shares the symbolism of the perfection and power of the circle.'[14] Robert Lawlor likewise says the pentagon was 'the symbol of life, particularly of human life'[15] and gives an illustration of man as the pentagon.

In the ritual of the temple, the high priest, representing the whole nation of Israel, went into the Holy of Holies once a year on the Day of Atonement to obtain expiation for the sins of the people. No one else was ever allowed into this Most Holy Place. He went through the pentagonal door as, so to speak, the pentagramal man, i.e. man in the process of being made perfect. The door into the perfect cube of the cosmos had to represent the shape of the perfect man. Although by New Testament times this door had been replaced by a curtain or veil, Christ as perfect high priest 'after the order of Melchizedek' (Heb.7:11) entered the Holy of Holies when the 'curtain of the temple was torn in two' (Luke 23:45). As it says in the letter to the Hebrews:

> But when Christ appeared as a high priest of the good things that have come ... he entered once and for all into the Holy Place taking ... his own blood, thus securing an external redemption (Heb.9:11f).

This connection between the perfect pentagramal man and the perfect pentagonal doorway is brought out by John Michell in *City of Revelation*, a profound study of the links between the temple and the New Jerusalem. Michell's scholarship is based on the evidence of gematria, another ancient numerical discipline in which every Hebrew and Greek letter corresponded to a number.[16] Speaking about the pentagon-pentagram relationship he makes an astonishing link between it and the gematria of the name of Jesus Christ (in Greek, *Iesous Christos*):

There is an obvious connection between the pentagram and the body of the canonical man crucified, which is confirmed in the golden section measurements of the human body, and the following circumstance could scarcely have been ignored by the founders of the Christian religion: that a square drawn on the height of a pentagon with a side measuring one unit has an area of 2.368, and 2368 is the number of the crucified man, Iesous Christos. In Fig 23 [see Fig.3.8. (b), p. 56] the horizontal dotted line, approximately coinciding with the upper limbs of the pentagram, divides the square into two rectangles so that the area of the upper rectangle is 888, Jesus, of the lower 1480, Christ.

That 2368, the most sacred number of the Christian cabalists, the sum of the values of the letter in the name of Jesus Christ, should be a thousand times the area of a square on the height of a pentagon measuring 1 unit on every side is a law of nature and not a contrivance of ancient geometers ... The sacred numbers are not merely from human choice: they are inherent in the structure of the universe and must recur to whoever studies the unifying science of cosmology.[17]

All that Michell says confirms that the pentagon-pentagram represented by the shape of the doorway into the Holy of Holies, was realized in the person and work of Jesus Christ.

The icons of Eden

It was not only the cubic shape of the New Jerusalem that St John took from the symbolism of the temple. His vision of a restored Eden, as described in Chapter 1, was also pictured in terms of its contents, for if we look at the sacred objects and wall carvings that were inside the temple, it is not difficult to see that they were stylized representations of the main features of the garden of Eden.

We are told that for the Holy Place, Solomon made 'the golden altar, the golden table for the bread of the Presence, the lamp-stands of pure gold, five on the south side and five on the north, before the inner sanctuary' (1Kings 7:48f). These were usually known as the altar of incense, the table of shewbread and the seven-branch candlesticks. The symbolism of these pieces of holy furniture has been seen by traditional scholarship almost exclusively in spiritual terms; the incense as prayer, the bread as the Bread of Life and the candlesticks as the Light of God.[18] While there is undoubted truth in such interpretations, they entirely obscure the original connection which all these objects had with nature; the gum and resin of incense with the fragrance of the forest,[19] the cereal offering of the shewbread with agricultural production,[20] and the candlesticks with the almond tree (Exod.25:31–40). It is these lamp-stands which point back most obviously to the garden of Eden because it was the almond tree which was the tree of life for the Hebrews.[21] As St John saw the tree of life standing in the midst of the New Jerusalem, so the Israelites saw an avenue of the same trees of life standing within the temple. In both cases they symbolized an earthly paradise and the message was one of harmony with nature. This is borne out by the clear ecological meaning of Ezekiel's vision of this same avenue of trees coming to life in the desert (Ezek.47:1–12, cf. Rev.22:1f).

The wall decorations of the Holy Place and the Holy of Holies agree with this Edenic interpretation because we are told that Solomon 'carved all the walls round about with carved figures of cherubim and palm trees and open flowers in the inner and the outer rooms' (1Kings 6:29). Although the actual appearance of the cherubim is uncertain, scholars agree that they were thought of as God's servants whose main job was to guard 'the Tree of Life in the Garden of Eden' (Gen.3:24).[22] This understanding of the cherubim as 'guardians of Paradise'[23] is developed by John Gray with specific reference to the temple wall carvings where he says: 'They guard the palm-tree as the tree of life,'[24] the date-palm being the tree of life for the nomads of the desert in the same way as the almond tree was for the Jews.[25]

There was nothing else in the temple except what it had been specifically built to house — the Ark of the Covenant. This box containing the Law stood in the centre of the Holy of Holies flanked by its two enormous protecting cherubim. In terms of our Eden imagery this symbolized the living presence of the Lord God in the midst of his creation (Gen.3:8).

As the structure of the temple expressed the perfect harmony of the cosmos in architectural proportions equivalent to those of the pure musical intervals, so its contents expressed the same universal harmony in its earthly form of the trees, food and fragrance of Eden. Like the New Jerusalem, the temple was a microcosm of the perfect harmony of heaven and earth. It is tragic that such a magnificent concept of oneness with God and nature should have been obscured for so long. At a time when we are reaping the bitter harvest of centuries of disrespect for nature, it is important that it should be recovered.

Jesus and the temple of his body

It is not hard to see why Jesus, Stephen and Paul were all what might be called 'temple-bashers.' The temple had been built as a paradigm of the whole of creation, but by New Testament times the Jews had obscured this cosmic dimension behind a plethora of ritualism and legalism. They had mistaken the sign for the thing signified. The temple had taken the place of creation as an object of reverence. The trials of Jesus and Stephen, and the arrest of Paul, all centred round their objection to this form of idolatry.

The inner reason for Jesus' hostility to the temple was not just that he was enraged by the corruption of those who 'were selling oxen and sheep and pigeons, and the money changers at their business' (John 2:14). It was also that, as C.F.D. Moule says, he represented in his own person 'the ultimate supersession of the cultus by the reality for which the cultus stands.'[26] When the Jews asked him what authority he had for driving the sacrificial animals and the money changers out of the temple courtyard, he said, 'Destroy this temple, and in three days I will raise it up.' The Jews of course did not understand because, as John explains, 'he spoke of the temple of his body' (John 2:19,21).

It was this antagonism to the temple as much as his open hostility to the scribes and Pharisees, which led to his eventual arrest and trial. As John Bowker points out, 'the *immediate* issue was concentrated on the extent to which Jesus had repudiated the Temple and, by implication, its authority.'[27]

Stephen and the temple of creation

The story of the arrest, trial and condemnation of Stephen is meant to be seen as a sequel to the trial and condemnation of Jesus. Like Jesus, Stephen was charged with blasphemy by men who were secretly planted to say: 'We have heard him speak blasphemous words against Moses and God' (Acts 6:11). As with Jesus, they also set up false witnesses who accused him of speaking against the law and the temple:

> This man never ceases to speak words against the holy place and the law; for we have heard him say that this Jesus of Nazareth will destroy this place, and will change the customs which Moses delivered to us (Acts 6:13f).

Jesus had remained silent before his accusers but Stephen made up for it by delivering the longest sermon recorded in the New Testament, apart from the Sermon on the Mount! He did not deny the charges but instead gave the Jewish council a lecture on Abraham, the patriarchs and Moses. It was a history lesson based on his belief that, just as their forefathers had turned away from Moses, the prophets and the law, they had now in their turn betrayed and murdered Jesus. This was his reply to the accusation that he spoke blasphemously against Moses. As regards the charge that he also spoke against the law, he maintained that the true law was to do with ethics and not animal sacrifices. He quoted Jeremiah and Amos to the effect that justice and righteousness were what the law really required, not burnt offerings and solemn assemblies (Acts 7:42f).

This was also his major contention with regard to the temple. Just as their forefathers had got along perfectly well without any slain beasts and sacrifices during the forty years in the wilderness, so Abraham, the patriarchs and Moses had all been close to God without needing any temple at all. From Moses to David all they had had was a tent of witness. It was only David who had 'asked leave to find a habitation for the God of Jacob' (Acts 7:46) which his son Solomon had built.

Stephen was telling the Jews that they had forgotten their history and had made secondary things primary. The faith of Abraham and the patriarchs had come long before the law. The law had come long before the temple. Their priorities were back to front. They needed to be reminded that, at the time of the building of the second temple, Isaiah had affirmed the more ancient and universal truth that God did not live in temples made with hands but rather that he lived in the length, breadth and height of the temple of his creation:

> Yet the Most High does not dwell in houses made
> with hands; as the prophet says:
> Heaven is my throne,
> and earth my footstool.

> What house will you build for me, says the Lord,
> or what is the place of my rest?
> Did not my hands make all things?
> (Acts 7:48–50; Isa.66:1f)

This particular quotation from Isaiah was Stephen's punchline. This was the scriptural text, which clinched his argument. A significant strand in the prophetic tradition supported this interpretation of Jewish history. Isaiah was only one of many who had said that just as God desired 'love not sacrifice' (Hos.6:6) so he also desired to be worshipped in the temple of his creation, not in houses made with hands.[28]

However true this understanding of the law and the prophets might have been, it sounded subversive to those who were committed to the cultus and not to the reality for which the cultus stood. As F.F. Bruch comments: 'Real or imagined belittling of the Temple was certain to rouse to fury both the city populace and the priestly party with their vested interests in the building and its cultus.'[29] Their reaction was predictable. As they had had little compunction in stoning the prophets and condemning Jesus, so they now made short work of this impudent disciple of the prophet Jesus who put faith, righteousness and the temple of creation before animal sacrifices, solemn assembly and Herod's temple.

Luke, the writer of Acts, obviously saw this sequel to the trial and death of Jesus as definitive of the differences between those who continued to follow the traditional understanding of Moses, the law and the temple, and those who reinterpreted this tradition in the light of Jesus, the new Moses, the law of the heart and the temple of creation. This theme is one of the most important in the Acts of the Apostles, and appears again most noticeably in the preaching and arrest of Paul.

Paul and the temple not made with hands

When Paul was on his missionary journeys attempting to convert the people of Athens, he spoke out as strongly against the altars and shrines of Greece as Stephen had done against the Jewish temple. Paul himself was a staunch believer in the concept of a national cultus centred on a sacred shrine (Acts 21:26; 24:11) but he was able to extend this concept to embrace a universalism based on God as the creator of all things and all people:

> The God who made the world and everything in it, being Lord of heaven and earth, does not live in shrines made by man, nor is he served by human hands, as though he needed anything, since he himself gives to all men life and breath and everything. And he made from one every nation of men to live on all the face of the earth, having determined allotted periods and the boundaries of their habitation, that they should seek God, in the hope that they might feel after him and find him. Yet he is not far from each of us for:
>
> 'In him we live and move and have our being;' as even some of your poets have said,
>
> 'For we are indeed his offspring.' (Acts 17:24–28)

Stephen had said to his accusers that their historical memory was too short. They had to go farther back into history, to the time before the temple, to see what the law was really about and to the time before the law to see what Abraham's faith was all about. Paul was now encouraging the Greeks to go even farther back than that, to the very beginning of creation when God had made not only everything in heaven and on earth but also all nations and the different countries in which they were to live. In spite of much scholarship which contends that this whole speech reflects a pantheistic view of the deity which is incompatible with the rest of Paul's teaching, I agree with Bertil Gärtner that this universal creationism was at the heart of his gospel for the Gentiles, as distinct from those apostles who remained to some extent bound by nationalistic Judaism.[30] It was also the basis of his belief that Jesus was not just the second Moses, but the second Adam as well.

Like Jesus and Stephen before him, Paul soon found himself in trouble back home for this universalist preaching. When he returned to Jerusalem the following year to tell the apostles about the success of his missionary journeys, only arrest by the Roman guards saved him from summary execution at the hands of the Jewish mob. Their almost uncontrollable violence towards him was based on the same grounds as that which had been shown towards Stephen and Jesus: 'This is the man who is teaching men everywhere against the people and the law and this place; moreover he has defiled this holy place' (Acts 21:28).

It is sobering to reflect that many contemporary Christians, with their pre-occupation with ecclesiastical buildings and lack of serious environmental concern, might have more in common with the Jews who defended the temple than with Jesus, Stephen and Paul. We too seem to be in grave danger of mistaking the sign for the thing signified, the church at the street corner for the temple of creation.

4. Cycles of Seven and the Jewish Festivals

So far in this enquiry we have been dealing with the biblical concept of cosmic space as expressed in the models of the New Jerusalem and Solomon's temple. We are now going to attempt to examine aspects of the Old Testament understanding of cosmic time, for only by so doing shall we gain enough background knowledge to see the universal dimension of Christ's ministry in a new light.

Bearing in mind all that we have already established, I believe it is possible to show that the harmony of space built into Solomon's Temple found an equivalent embodiment in the Israelites' annual divisions of time. The same principles of number and ratio which we have seen expressed in the spatial proportions of the temple, were also expressed in the times and seasons of their calendrical year. This is most apparent in the timing of the annual festivals, which put great emphasis on intervals involving the number seven.

The number seven occurs 287 times in the Bible, and is one of the most prevalent numbers in the scriptures. Many well-known instances of its occurrence spring to mind such as Namaan being told to wash seven times in the Jordan; Jesus telling Peter to forgive seventy times seven, and the seven churches in Revelation. In fact, there are so many famous instances that, as Maurice Farbridge aptly remarks: 'It would indeed be a work of supererogation to go over all the passages of the Bible where it occurs in order to make out that it has deep significance.'[1] Many scholars would go further, agreeing with Ethelbert Bullinger that it 'is used as *no other number* is,'[2] that it symbolized something holy,[3] sacred,[4] and spiritually perfect.[5]

Yet despite its prevalence and evident importance, at no point do the scriptures tell us explicitly why this should be so. As with so many aspects of the scriptural use of numbers, we have been left to work out this secret for ourselves. Why has the number seven been thought of as holy, sacred and spiritually perfect? What is its deep significance? In attempting to answer these riddles, we shall also lay bare some of the mysteries of cosmic time in the Bible.

The lunar quarter

At first glance the answer does not seem hard to find because seven is usually understood to be a lunar number and most scholars would agree with Farbridge that 'amongst the Semites the symbolical character of seven originated with the division of the lunar month into quarters.'[6] Seven is the nearest whole number to a quarter of the moon's cycle of $29^1/_2$ days. As we have already discovered 'semitic symbolism is based on the belief that there is an analogy between all activities in heaven and everything on earth.'[7] It therefore followed that since 'the number seven was regarded as sacred in heaven, it must also be held as sacred on earth.'[8]

This explanation certainly agrees with much of the biblical record, for the moon was clearly important to the Hebrews and is referred to far more frequently than any other heavenly body except the sun. The new moon is often mentioned together with the sabbath (for example, 2Kings 4:23, Amos 8:5, Hos.2:13, Isa.1:13) and was often kept as a feast day. It ranked second only to the sun and was singled out as a special wonder of creation when all the other stars were undifferentiated:

> When I look at the heavens, the work of thy fingers the moon and the stars which thou has established (Psalm 8:3).

But above all it would appear that the moon was important in Israel because it had been made 'to mark the seasons' (Psalm 104:19). It had been appointed as the 'lesser light' to rule the night, just as the sun, the 'greater light,' had been appointed to rule the day. Together with the sun it had been made for 'signs and for seasons and for days and years' as the creation story makes clear:

> And God said, 'Let there be lights in the firmament of the heavens to separate the day from the night; and let them be for signs and for seasons and for days and years, and let them be lights in the firmament of the heavens to give light upon the earth.' And it was so. And God made the two great lights, the greater light to rule the day, and the lesser light to rule the night; he made the stars also (Gen.1:14–16).

The central importance of the moon in the measurement of time was basic to the consciousness of early man throughout the world as he began to understand the mysterious workings of the chronometer of the heavens. As J.C. Cooper states: 'The moon is universally symbolic of the rhythm of cyclic time ... As periodic re-creation it is Time and measurement, time being first measured by lunar phases.'[9]

It was for this reason that seven was used throughout the Bible as a basic unit of time.[10] There were sand and water clocks and sexagesimal arithmetic to measure the minutes and hours,[11] but the larger units of time were calculated by means of the cycles of the sun and moon. The sun was the clock for the days and years and the moon was the clock for the weeks and months. The two together gave light and regulated the calendar.

The Genesis story speaks of the moon being 'for signs and for seasons' which in the New English Bible is translated 'for festivals and for seasons,' in the Jerusalem Bible as for 'festivals,' and in the Today's English Version as for 'religious festivals.' These translations indicate that Hebrew festivals as well as the weeks and months were regulated by the moon. They also explain why the number seven is so conspicuous in the list of the annual feasts as they are given first in Exodus, then in Numbers and Deuteronomy and finally, in their most comprehensive form, in Leviticus.[12] Turning to the latter, it is apparent that the time scheme of the festivals is almost completely made up of cycles of seven.

The Jewish festivals

In Leviticus (23) the first appointed feast was the sabbath of solemn rest 'on the seventh day.' The second was on the fourteenth (i.e. 7×2) day of the first month. This was the Passover, which was immediately followed on the fifteenth day by the feast of Unleavened Bread, which lasted for seven days. During these eight days the people remembered their miraculous escape from slavery in Egypt. The next six verses (9–14) speak of the feast of the First Sheaf of the barley harvest, which took place on the second day of the feast of Unleavened Bread.[13] Verses 15–21 then give details of the feast of the wheat harvest, the feast of Weeks. This had to be celebrated exactly *seven* full weeks after the feast of the First Sheaf:

And you shall count from the morrow after the sabbath, from the day that you brought the sheaf of the wave offering; seven full weeks they shall be, counting fifty days to the morrow after the seventh sabbath; then you shall present a cereal offering of new grain to the Lord (Lev.23:15f).

Having enumerated the feasts of the seventh day and the seventh week, the next on the list was the feast of Trumpets, which marked the beginning of the seventh month:

In the seventh month, on the first day of the month, you shall observe a day of solemn rest, a memorial proclaimed with blast of trumpets (Lev.23:24).

As mentioned above, each new moon was kept as a feast day by the Israelites. The seventh is the only one listed because it was the most important. It was the new moon of the harvest month in a calendar year, which began with the spring.[14]

The Day of Atonement came next (vv.26–32). This was on the tenth day of the seventh month. It was a day, which symbolized *at-one-ment* or reconciliation, not only with the cycles of seven but also with the law as signified by the tenth day. On this portentous occasion the High Priest entered the Holy of Holies on behalf of the nation, and the people confessed their sins, their 'dissonances,' and got back in tune with the cosmic harmony of God. N.H. Snaith, in his commentary *Leviticus and Numbers*, confirms this harmonic and celebratory interpretation when he says:

Originally this day was a day of great rejoicing, and it was one of the two days in the year when the maidens of Jerusalem went out to dance in the vineyards, apparently a betrothal dance ... The penitential sorrow of the Day of Atonement is a later development.[15]

The final festival of the year was the feast of Booths or Tabernacles, on the fifteenth day of the seventh month, which lasted seven days (Lev.23:33–43). This was the final harvest-home for the agricultural produce, especially for the fruit, the olive and the grape. It was a joyful time of thanksgiving, which ended with prayers for the autumnal rains and the next year's sowing.[16]

This obsession with the rhythm of seven in cyclic time was carried on beyond the feasts which marked the seven days, the seven weeks and the seventh month, into larger cycles of the years. Leviticus (25) lists two more kinds of sabbath which were both based on the rhythm of seven, but in these cases the unit of time was not seven days or seven weeks, but seven years and seven weeks of years. The first of these was the seventh or sabbath year, the Sabbatical, which was instituted as a year of rest for all agricultural land:

> The Lord said to Moses: 'Say unto the people of Israel, When you come into the land which I give you, the land shall keep a Sabbath to the Lord. Six years you shall sow your field, and six years you shall prune your vineyard, and gather in its fruits; but in the seventh year there shall be a sabbath of solemn rest for the land, a sabbath to the Lord; you shall not sow your field or prune your vineyard.' (Lev.25:1–4)

The second of these was the fiftieth or Jubilee year which was measured in exactly the same way as the feast of Weeks only in years instead of weeks, but there was also much more to it than that:

> And you shall count seven weeks of years, seven times seven years, so that the time of the seven weeks of years shall be to you forty-nine years. Then you shall send abroad the loud trumpet on the tenth day of the seventh month; on the day of atonement you shall send forth the trumpet throughout all your land. And you shall hallow the fiftieth year, and proclaim liberty throughout the land to all its inhabitants; it shall be a jubilee for you, when each of you shall return to his family. A jubilee shall that fiftieth year be to you; in it you shall neither sow nor reap what grows of itself, nor gather the grapes from the undressed vines. For it shall be a jubilee; it shall be holy to you. (Lev.25:8–12)

This fiftieth year was the ultimate expression of seven-ness and was very unlike the modern understanding of 'jubilee,' meaning anniversary. Firstly, it was a second successive year of rest for the land following on from the Sabbatical of the forty-ninth year.[17] Secondly, it was concerned with the enactment of socio-economic legislation regarding the release of slaves from their terms of service, the cancellation of debts,

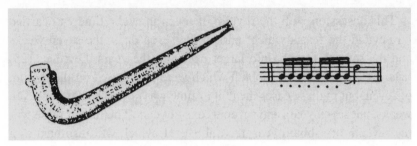

Fig.4.1. (a) The shofar, *and Fig.4.1. (b) The* teru'ah.

and the return of property to its original ownership. Thirdly, the Hebrew word *yobel*, from which jubilee is derived, denotes a specific kind of ram's horn which was blown uniquely on that occasion. The Year of Jubilee, *shanat ha-yobel*, therefore literally meant the year which was announced by blasts on the horn. In the Letter to the Hebrews (9) this *yobel* horn blast is described as the *shofar teru'ah*, the *shofar* being the generic word for ram's horn. The difference between the use of the words *yobel* and *shofar* in this context is clarified by Alfred Sendrey, in *Music in Ancient Israel*, who says that the *yobel* was 'the metal sound bell, which could be applied to the *shofar*. It may therefore be assumed with reasonable certainty that the term *yobel* implied an instrument put together of several parts, the most important of which was apparently the sound bell.'[18]

The planets and the Great Bear

The Sabbath day, Passover, Unleavened Bread, First Sheaf, Weeks, Trumpets, Atonement, Tabernacles, the Sabbatical and Jubilee year, were thus all festivals which were fitted into a concept of time in which the number seven and its multiples were central. Indeed, the dating of these feasts was so dominated by this number that it almost appears as if the thing that is really being celebrated is the number seven itself, as if it was indeed some sort of sacred entity. Even so it would seem that this obsession with seven had got rather out of hand and that such an overwhelming concentration on a number only associated with the moon's quarter was unwarranted. The 'lesser light' might well have been made for the appointment of festivals as well as 'for signs and for seasons,' but need it have been taken to quite such lengths? Why for instance is it always the moon's quarter that is taken as the basic unit of time? Why not half or three quarters, that is, fourteen or twenty-one days? And why are the feast of Weeks and the Jubilee year both reckoned by the computation of seven times seven plus one, when neither forty-nine nor fifty are numbers which relate easily to the moon's cycles? Most pertinent of all, what possible connection can there be between lunar periods and either seven weeks or fifty years? This last question, in particular, prompts the suspicion that the number seven may be so pervasive in the scriptures not only because it is approximately a quarter of the lunar cycle, but also because it had some more profound significance. Once again, although they don't say why, scholars agree that seven times seven was 'a specially sacred number.'[19] Could it be that despite the foregoing arguments, the number seven was not *primarily* a lunar number after all?

The fact that the ancient world recognized seven planets could perhaps have been another reason why this number was considered to be so important, but the references to any heavenly body other than the sun and moon are so rare in the Bible that it does not seem likely, in spite of strong arguments to the contrary by some such as Robert Graves in *The White Goddess*.[20]

This also applies to the seven stars of the Great Bear which according to scholars, such as Geoffrey Ashe, in *The Ancient Wisdom*, was the original source of the sacredness of the heptad.[21] The constellation of Ursa Major in early times was considered to be indestructible because, throughout the year, it never left the northern sky. It could always be seen moving round the pole and so was associated with the *axis mundi*, the axle of the universe. According to this cosmology, the *axis mundi* gave access to cosmic and divine power so that the temples and holy mountains of many cultures, such as Mount Meru in India, Nippur in Sumer and Safon in Lebanon, were believed to have been built at its base.[22]

There are a few references in the Bible which link Mount Zion with this concept, most notably Psalm 48 where 'Mount Zion, in the far north, the city of the great king' appears to be a reference to this universal cosmic mountain. But although God's chariot appeared to Ezekiel 'out of the north' (Ezek.1:4) and Amos spoke of God as: 'He who made the Pleiades [AV: the seven stars] and Orion' (Amos 5:8) and Jesus Christ had seven stars in his right hand (Rev.1:16), these and a few other indirect references, are not enough on their own to justify such an overt preponderance of the number seven throughout the scriptures. If neither the seven planets nor the seven stars of the Great Bear are enough in themselves to explain this phenomenon, then what other concept is there that would be large enough and universal enough to do so?

Seven scales and seven octaves

There is only one direction in which I believe an answer to this question is likely to be found and that is in the direction of music. Music, as we saw in the last chapter, was known to consist of harmonious sounds equivalent to simple numerical ratios. I do not think it is going too far to say that it was this concept of musical harmony, at the heart of ancient cosmology, which was both mirrored in and confirmed by the seven planets and the seven stars of Ursa Major.

As well as being the nearest whole number to a quarter of the moon's cycle, and to a lesser extent the number of the planets and the Great Bear, seven was also known to be the number of notes in the musical scale. This had been discovered on the monochord as early as 3000 BC, and from it a theory of the harmony of all things had been developed as already indicated.[23] This musical fact, that there were seven notes — not eight or six — corresponded to the celestial fact that there were approximately seven days in the lunar quarter, seven planets and seven stars in the Great Bear. The lunar quarter, the planets and the Great Bear thus all confirmed a theory of music, in which the number seven was seen to be the number of harmony on the earth and in the heavens. According to this theory the number of notes in the musical scale corresponded to the number of days in the week, and a complete octave was equivalent to the eight days from sabbath to sabbath.

If the predominance of seven throughout the scriptures, and particularly in the timing of the festivals, came not primarily from the lunar quarter but from a theory of musical harmony in the microcosm and the macrocosm, it would explain why this number seems to have a life of its own, so universal is its application and symbolism. If it was known as the number of perfection and completion because it was the number of notes in the complete musical scale, then it would automatically coincide with the number associated with the moon's quarter and give to it a much greater importance than it would otherwise have had. This would explain why the obsession with cycles of seven seems to be so predominant in the dating of the festivals, especially those that depended on having to count seven times seven plus one, that is, the feast of Weeks and the Jubilee year. For what possible connection could the numbers forty-nine and fifty — taken as weeks, or years — have with the lunar cycle?[24] The fact that it was seven times seven that had to be counted, suggests a meaning that might be connected more with seven musical scales than with seven quarters of the moon. If seven times seven plus one was meant to be understood not as a *lunar* but as a *musical* number, then the meaning of these numbers becomes obvious because forty-nine is the number of notes in seven complete scales and fifty is the number in seven full octaves.

Supposing that this musical meaning does explain why seven times seven plus one had to be counted to fix the date of the feast of Weeks and the year of Jubilee, what difference does it make? How does it help to clarify the meaning of the number seven? Are seven octaves musically significant? Only if we can find some profound musical importance in the number fifty will this interpretation seem to be a reasonable one.

The Pythagorean Comma

If we look deeply into harmonic theory, this is precisely what we find. Seven octaves or fifty notes are associated with a mathematical anomaly known as 'Pythagoras's Comma' which, like almost everything else attributed to that gentleman, had exercised the minds of mathematicians and musicians for many centuries before he lived. This puzzle consisted of the fact that the measurements of seven octaves and twelve musical fifths, which should have been exactly the same, were found to have a noticeable discrepancy between them.

An octave is measured by doubling the original number which, if taken as 1 gives the number 128 for the seventh octave (i.e. 1, 2, 4, 8, 16, 32, 64, 128). A fifth is measured by multiples of 1.5 which makes the twelfth fifth come to the number 129.746 (i.e. 1.5, 2.25, 3.375, 5.062, 7.594, 11.39, 17.06, 25.629, 38.443, 57.665, 86.498, 129.746). Herbert Whone, in *The Hidden Face of Music*, describes the strange phenomenon, which becomes apparent to anyone who is attempting to construct a total key system in perfect fifths. In this case he is starting from the central point of middle C:

> With the central locking point established, the construction of the total key or locking system operates not unpredictably in series

of fives. Moving up from middle C in perfect fifths we arrive at all the sharp keys, G, D, A, E, B, etc, and moving downwards in the same way we arrive at all the flat keys, F, B♭, E♭, A♭ etc. The whole cycle embraces all the twelve half tones of the diatonic scale, and gives a system of scale which ... represent all possible type differentiations in a concrete whole.

But in this system there is a strange phenomenon — and it is connected with mathematics. Twelve steps of a perfect fifth in the harmonic system upwards or downwards from middle C, as we have said, brings us back to a C seven octaves (seven signifying completion) distant from it. We can ascertain that the frequency of the upper C is 128 times that of the lower one. But if we take the ratio of the perfect fifth (3:2 or 1.5) we find that our twelve steps increased by a factor of 1.5 bring us to the figure 129.75. The difference is of course known as the comma of Pythagoras. It is a strange phenomenon and a mathematical imponderable in which the octave closes the lock of predictable order and in which the fifth overshooting the mark opens the door to an infinity of frequencies.[25]

If this mathematical and harmonic enigma, known as the 'Pythagorean Comma,' makes the seventh octave so important, then a musical inter-pretation of the seven times seven plus one, written into the compu-tation of the feast of Weeks and the Jubilee year, would seem much more likely than a lunar explanation. According to this theory, fifty would be significant because it was related to this Pythagorean musical Comma, not because it was related to the moon's phases. But although this is an intriguing possibility, it raises the deeper question why this Pythagorean Comma was so important that it had to be celebrated in the dating procedure of these two festivals? If this ancient concept of cosmic harmony worked with a theory of correspondences between the earth and the heavens, there would still need to be something equally anomalous in the heavens to justify the conspicuous inclusion of the number fifty in the calendar. The question must therefore be put: what was there in the time-cycles of the heavenly bodies that corresponded to the musical discrepancy between the seventh octave and the twelfth fifth?

Tuning the moon to the sun

I believe the answer to this is very straightforward and lies simply in the basic discrepancy between the lunar and the solar year. It was this fundamental celestial anomaly which, in my opinion, corresponded to the musical discrepancy of the Pythagoran Comma. The question we must now ask is, how was this worked out?

Jack Finegan, in *Handbook of Biblical Chronology*, shows that there were two main influences on the Hebrew's reckoning of the calendar. The first was the Egyptian-Phoenician calendar and the second, the Babylonian calendar. The Egyptian was essentially a solar system and the Babylonian, a luni-solar one. He says that both of these considerably influenced the formation of the Israelite calendar and both used a standardized month of thirty days, which was *not* closely related to the moon. In his section 'The Israelite Calendar' he says:

> It is perhaps not without significance that it is precisely the first two months of the fall and the first two of spring of which the names are preserved in the Old Testament. These are not only times of special importance in Palestinian agriculture but also the times of the two equinoxes. It will also be remembered that in the early period the day was probably reckoned from the morning. These facts suggest that the orientation of this calendar was primarily towards the sun: the rising of the sun began the day; the equinoxes were the turning points of the year. If this was the case then, in the lack of other evidence, the guess may be hazarded that the months were not tied closely to the phases of the moon but were units of the solar year, probably thirty days in length, as in the 'schematic' calendars of Egypt and Mesopotamia, and that the resultant shortage of about five days was simply made up by the insertion of additional days at the end of the year.[26]

He concludes his argument by saying that 'it seems entirely likely that at least from the time of Solomon and under the influence of Egypt and Phoenicia, the calendar of Israel was a schematic solar calendar.'[27]

There are many complicating factors regarding the biblical calendar arising from, among other things, the later Babylonian influence, as Finegan goes on to demonstrate. However, if we accept this part of his argument then we may take it that, at least from the time of Solomon to the exile, the Hebrews were most probably operating with a calendar of twelve standardized lunar months of thirty days and were not closely adhering to twelve lunar months of $29^1/_2$ days. Their *lunar* year was thus 360 (i.e. 12 × 30 days) long and not 354 (i.e. 12 × $29^1/_2$). If this were so, then they had approximately five extra days to add in to make up the full solar year of $365^1/_4$ days.

As far as I can see, it may well have been these five extra days, which corresponded to the musical discrepancy of the Pythagorean Comma, as a simple piece of arithmetic indicates. If we divide 129.746 (the twelfth fifth) by 128 (the seventh octave), we get 1.0136433. Therefore, 1 to 1.0136433 is the ratio of the two numbers. If we wish to convert this ratio into degrees on a 360-degree circle we must multiply 1.0136433 by 360. This gives 364.91158. If we multiply the difference, i.e. 0.136433 by 360, we get 4.911575. In other words the Pythagorean Comma is equivalent to 4.9 degrees or 4.9 days in the year, thus increasing the total length of the year from 360 to 364.9 days. I find it reasonable to conclude that this 'comma' of 4.9 was taken to be equivalent to the five extra days, which made up an approximation to the full solar year.

In coming to this conclusion I find myself in disagreement with Ernest McClain who, in *The Myth of Invariance*, makes the Comma equivalent to 7.2 degrees.[28] I also wonder how Alain Daniélou, in his magisterial work *An Introduction to the Study of Musical Scales*, can say that the correspondence between the Comma and the sun-moon discrepancy is a *precise* one:

> In reality, the physical laws which are applicable to sound are not particular to them, but are those which regulate all the normal rhythms of the Universe, and those 'positive' minds, which smile at such conceptions, might be very embarrassed if Saturday did not come every eighth day, if the days no longer had 24 hours (12+12), the hours 60 minutes, and if the relation of the sun and the moon no longer formed for us a cycle of 12 months with, precisely, a slight difference comparable to that of 12 fifths and seven octaves.[29]

I find that I cannot accept what Daniélou appears to be saying without the qualifications that by '12 months' he means 360 not 354 days (i,e, standardized, not lunar months), and that by 'with, precisely, a slight difference comparable to that of 12 fifths and seven octaves' he does *not* mean that the comparison is exact. I do not see how he can use the word 'precisely' when the Comma is equivalent to only 4.9 days and the approximate discrepancy between the lunar and the solar year, even taking it as a schematic 360 days, is 5.25. Even with the Comma there is still a discrepancy of approximately 0.35 days.

Nevertheless, I believe that the comparison was close enough to be taken as a correspondence between heaven and earth, on the 'as above, so below' principle, and that it was sufficiently exact to be taken to represent the ancient belief that the universe sang and was constructed in accordance with harmony. I believe it was a sufficiently important aspect of the ancient wisdom to be incorporated into the Holiness Code of the Book of the Covenant of Leviticus, and that the injunctions to count fifty days to mark the feast of Weeks and fifty years to mark the year of Jubilee can best be explained by means of this cosmology.

Confirmation of this opinion regarding the extra five days has come in recent years from the researches of Robert Temple conducts a most extensive examination into the importance of the Comma in the ancient world. He says that in Egyptian Cosmology it was known as 'the tiny gap,' and that its minute fraction of 1.014 represented the difference between an ideal year of 360 days and the true year of 365 days, 5 hours and 48 minutes. It was evidently 'the most important secret number of the gods.'

Their god Thoth was known as 'the eighth, who completed the Octave' and regarding the Fifth he says:

> The musical fifth was represented by five gods including Isis and Osiris, known as 'The Five' and they re-presented the five extra days which were added on to 360 to make 365; the fraction of a day added to them to give the true year was called Horus.[30]

All Temple's prodigious research not only confirms my calculations, but also shows that in all probability the Hebrews derived it from the wisdom of Egypt, which they took with them at the time of the Exodus.

We can now understand why the year of Jubilee was called the year of the *yobel*, the amplified ram's horn, and why it was announced by repeated blasts on that instrument. For this was the year which celebrated the completion of the cycle of seven 'octave-years.' It also celebrated the completion of the cycle of twelve 'fifth-years' and the discrepancy between the two.

The fundamental musical anomaly also had deep theological meaning in the ancient world, for it was evidently seen as a metaphor for both the discord of man's sinfulness, and also of the hope of his ultimate resurrection. David Tame, in *The Secret Power of Music*, has an appendix on 'The Mystery of Pythagoras' Comma' in which he clearly defines these two profound spiritual interpretations of the Comma. Firstly, he speaks about it as a symbol of man's fallen-ness:

> The comma produces huge cosmological, as well as practical, implications and results. Since this system of calculating twelve notes (i.e. by perfect fifths) does not perfectly complete the octave, the specific twelve pitches it produces are imperfect for use together in harmony. They do not perfectly harmonize since they do not divide the octave into perfectly accurate divisions of twelve as, say, the hours of a clock do perfectly divide a clock face. Yet to adjust their slight pitch discrepancies in order to produce perfect harmony would render each note imperfect as an interval of a fifth, or as a ratio of 3:2. The perfecting of their musical system was paramount to the ancients, for their music had to harmonize with the eternal laws of the universe. Therefore the perfect ratio of 3:2 and its interval of a perfect fifth were regarded as sacred and inviolable. If the system resulted, as it did, in the harmony of mortal music being imperfect, then this had to be borne as a manifest symbol of man's fall from grace, and of the inherent imperfection of the non-heavenly realm of time and space.[31]

He then goes on to speak of the other, complementary spiritual significance of the Comma, that of the hope of ultimate resurrection:

> Though the comma may be a symbol of the imperfection of man's mortal state, the very same comma simultaneously provides the way back to the original state of perfection. For the comma is not a slight interval *less* than seven octaves, but *in excess* of them. In the ancient world, this fact was widely conceived as a symbol of *renewal*. The cycle of twelve perfect fifths did not *close* and

finish a cycle of seven octaves, but exceeded it, and thus, as it were, spiralled *upward*. There is evidence that this upward spiral of renewal was mystically associated with the widespread ancient myth of the phoenix, the archetypal 'bird' which is resurrected from its own ashes. Pythagoras' Comma, then, can be seen as God's own engram written into the very law of the universe and of physics. And it is by the nature of this engram that man is heir to the promise of eventual resurrection and ascension out of the dim caverns of mortality.[32]

Such passages demonstrate convincingly why the Comma was considered to be so spiritually, as well as musically and cosmically, important. Tame impressively confirms my belief that the Israelite calendar embodies this spirituality in its computation of the feast of Weeks and the Jubilee year. This is particularly so with regard to the latter, the *shanat ha-yobel*, the year of the *yobel*. The fact that the Jubilee year was announced by repeated blasts on the *yobel* on the Day of Atonement indicates a close correspondence with 'Pythagorean' cosmology. For this year of release was proclaimed on the most sacred of Jewish musical instruments by a series of repeated blasts on the *fundamental* and *fifth* notes! It was quite literally the musical expression of all that the ancient world believed about their spirituality and its relation to cosmic harmony.

The 'octave' year of twelve 'semitone' months

This basic correspondence between the music of the earth and the music of the heavens indicates that the positioning of the seven major Jewish festivals in the spring, early summer and autumn was most probably based not only on the seasons of the agricultural year and the equinoxes, but also on a musical division of the calendar in which each month represented the semitone of an octave. This is certainly the contention of David Tame:

It was believed that the twelve Tones really did express themselves individually to a greater degree according to the month of the year, the time of day, and so forth. A particular Tone 'sounded' more prominently in a particular month, and during a particular hour of the day.[33]

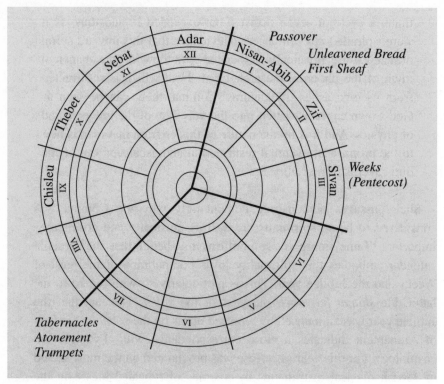

Fig.4.2. The festivals as the minor triad.

If this was indeed the case in Israel then Passover, Unleavened Bread and First Sheaf would, in the first month, be equivalent to the first tone, that is, the fundamental or tonic; the feast of Weeks, or Pentecost, as it was later called, in the third month, would be equivalent to a minor third, and Trumpets, Atonement and Tabernacles, in the seventh month, would be equivalent to the seventh semitone counting from the tonic, that is, the fifth, the dominant. Is it more than coincidence that these three notes form the minor triad? Could this be the origin of the frequent recurrence of the minor triad in Israeli folk music to this day?

It might also be possible on this analysis to speculate that the feast of Trumpets was held on the first day of the seventh month, not only because it marked the beginning of the harvest month and the ecclesiastical New Year, but also because it celebrated the month of the seventh semitone, the fifth — the very note which was the dominant note of the trumpets themselves! By the same analogy, the year of Jubilee would be ushered in on the tenth day of the seventh month not only because it was Old New Year's Day,[34] but also because that day symbolized the coming together of the number seven, representing harmony, and the number ten, representing the law. The proclamation of freedom for the slaves and the ending of leaseholds on property would be the social expression of this harmonious law. The blasts on the ram's horn would be blown to celebrate the dominant harmonic, as on the feast of Trumpets, but this time the metal sound bell would have been added which turned the *shofar* into the *yobel* and greatly amplified the instrument's sound, as befitted the greater occasion.

The tenth day of the seventh month of the fiftieth year, was thus the moment of supreme at-one-ment with the rhythms and cycles of God as expressed in his cosmos. The Day of Atonement, which ushered in the year of Jubilee, symbolized *par excellence* the tuning of all things on earth to the harmony of all things in heaven. It epitomized an obsession with harmony which is evident throughout all the feasts and festivals of the Levitical year, and in the incidence of the number seven throughout the Bible. It was because of its centrality to this harmonic cosmology that I believe the number seven came to be thought of as holy, sacred and spiritually perfect.

This comprehensive concept of harmony was intended to be put into practice throughout the whole of life and to bring about harmonious relationships between God, his people and his creation. All the feasts and festivals were understood to be the *beats* of rhythms, which were supposed to be resonating concordantly throughout the land all the time. The temple had been built to express these rhythms in space. The festivals were appointed to express them in time. The whole of the law was thus designed to express them in the continuum of space-time, so that all people and all things should always be in tune, in time, and in phase with each other, nature and God.

We shall see how this interpretation of the Jewish festivals, particularly with regard to Weeks or Pentecost and Jubilee, will help us rediscover the cosmic dimension in the ministry of Jesus Christ.

5. The Pulse of the Universe

Having threaded our way through some of the complexities of Old Testament time-cycles and arrived at what is, I hope, a reasonable hypothesis regarding the cosmology behind the Israelite calendar, it is time to capitalize on our findings. Now that we have learnt something about the background, we can begin to look at the ministry of Jesus, particularly at what is usually known as 'The Mission of the Seventy' (Luke 10:1–24).

In the last chapter the two most difficult questions we raised about the Hebrew calendar were: why did Leviticus command that seven full weeks, or fifty days, be counted from the feast of the First Sheaf, in order to compute the correct day for the celebration of the feast of Weeks (Lev.23:15f); and why was the same procedure enjoined, counting not days but weeks of years in order to observe the correct year for the Jubilee (Lev.25:8–23)? The answer we arrived at was that the $7 \times 7 + 1$ that had to be counted on both these occasions could not be completely explained by assuming that biblical scholars had been right when they had traditionally associated the number seven primarily with an approximation to a quarter of the moon's monthly cycle of $29^1/_2$ days. Rather, we came to the conclusion that the number seven referred, in the first instance, to the musical scale of seven major tones, and that the numbers forty-nine and fifty refer to seven scales and seven octaves respectively.

We then went on to explain the theory of the Pythagorean Comma and its approximate correspondence with the differential between the lunar and the solar year. We assumed that the Israelite calendar was strongly influenced in pre-exilic times by the Mesopotamian, Egyptian and Phoenician calendars, which were basically solar, and had twelve schematic months of thirty days, making up a 360 day year. We calculated that the Pythagorean Comma of ratio 129.746 to 128 was equivalent to 4.9 degrees and these 4.9 degrees did duty for the five days, which made up the full solar year of 365, to the nearest day. We realized that this was not a precise equivalence because it still fell short of the actual solar year of $365^1/_4$ days by approximately 0.35 of a day, but nevertheless we held that it was *taken* to be so by the ancients in their theory of cosmic harmony — 'as above, so below.'

The mission of the seventy or seventy-two

We have assumed that the 4.9 degrees of the Pythagorean Comma to be equivalent to the five extra days that made up the full solar year. If we reckon therefore that the 4.9 was equivalent to these five days, then we may also assume that these five days were $1/_{72}$ of the year, since 360 divided by 5 is 72. The ratio of the Pythagorean Comma to the year may thus be taken as 1 to 72.

If you read the New English Bible you will notice that in Luke (10:1&7) the number 72 is mentioned: 'After this the Lord appointed a further seventy-two and sent them on ahead of him in pairs ...' etc, and 'The seventy-two came back jubilant ...' etc. You may never have had this small detail drawn to your attention before, especially if you have been used to the AV and the RSV, for both of these translations use the number seventy and not seventy-two, and have thus given rise to the traditional title of this passage 'The Mission of the Seventy' In the footnote of the RSV it says: 'Other ancient authorities read *seventy-two*,' and the footnote in the NEB says: 'Some witnesses read *seventy*.' From other recent translations such as the Jerusalem Bible, Good News for Modern Man and the New International Version it is clear that seventy-two has now become the more acceptable rendering. Why should this be so? Why should most modern versions opt for seventy-two rather than seventy? Does that mean that seventy-two is the more authentic? There is a deeper question, which is: why should Jesus have a mission of the seventy or seventy-two at all? Wasn't the mission of the twelve apostles enough? Why either seventy or seventy-two?

Turning to a number of commentaries I found that some saw no particular significance in either number,[1] but most thought that the number seventy traditionally represented all the nations of the world (as in Gen.10), and that Jesus was symbolically inaugurating his mission to the Gentile world.[2] Some of these also thought that Jesus, as the second Moses, needed to have seventy elders to share his Spirit and ministry, just as the first Moses had before him.[3] The analogy between this and the ministry of our present-day churches would be that the twelve apostles were like the Roman Catholics and the Anglo-Catholics, while the seventy elders were all like good free churchmen, the former representing the hierarchy and the latter the ordinary working chaps! Be that as it may, I noticed that commentators varied considerably regarding the use of the number seventy or seventy-two. For instance, E. Earle Ellis, although he admitted that he didn't know for certain which number was the more authentic, went on to stress the importance of the number, which he assumed was seventy not seventy-two:

> The number had a weighty pedigree in Old Testament and Late Jewish tradition. There were seventy Gentile nations (Gen.10), seventy Israelites going into Egypt as the seed of the future people of God (Exod.1:5), seventy elders who accompanied Moses upon the holy mount and who received a portion of his prophetic spirit (Exod.24:1; Num.11:25). A similar number (plus the high priest) composed the Sanhedrin, the ruling representatives of the nation of Israel. It is highly probably that in the present context the number is symbolic and theologically significant.[4]

Unfortunately he did not go on to speculate as to what that symbolic and theological significance might have been. G.H.P. Thompson was equally undecided except that he included two extra elders, Eldad and Medad, who do in fact bring the number of the free churchmen up to seventy-two: 'Seventy, or 'seventy-two' (RSV margin; the manuscript evidence is divided) could be reminiscent of the seventy or seventy-two (if Eldad and Medad are included) elders who were appointed to assist Moses in the leadership of Israel (Num.11:10–31).'[5]

In an earlier commentary by John Martin Creed, I found a very interesting observation which suggested that seventy-two might have been the more authentic number. He argues that:

> There would be a tendency to make 72 into a round number. Similar confusion between 70 and 72 occurs in Gen X, (the numbers of the peoples) as between [the Hebrew and the Septuagint]; likewise in the traditional number of the Greek translators of the O.T.[6]

This last reference, to the Septuagint, we shall come to in a moment. His belief that 'there would be a tendency to make 72 into a round number' rang a bell with me because I could imagine that seventy might well have become shorthand for seventy-two. Another commentator, E.J. Tinsley, strengthened me in the conviction of this likelihood. Tinsley appears to have little doubt about seventy-two being the original reading:

Seventy-two is the number given in the Greek translation of the Hebrew Old Testament, the Septuagint, for the nations of the world in Genesis 10, and Numbers 11:24,26 seems to indicate seventy-two as the number of Moses' elders. Most probably this is the original reading, and 'seventy' crept in later because of its more common use as a symbol for something universal.[7]

According to Tinsley 'seventy crept in later because of its more common use as a symbol for something universal.' I can just see seventy creeping in stealthily and pushing out poor old seventy-two!

Finally, in an attempt to settle this point, I consulted Bruce Metzger's summary of all the primary sources of these texts, but noted his inconclusive opinion that 'the number of Jesus' disciples referred to in Luke 10 cannot be determined with confidence.'[8] However, in *A Textual Commentary on the Greek New Testament*, where he repeats his belief that the 'two' of seventy-two should only be printed in brackets, I observed that Kurt Aland disagreed. The substance of his disagreement is that seventy-two appears in so few texts compared with seventy that 'it is astonishing that the reading *ebdomekonta duo* occurs at all in 10.1 and 17, and that it has such strong support.' Such strong support he says, would normally be taken to mean that it was the original reading. He then amplifies Creed and Tinsley's point about the rounding down of seventy-two to seventy:

If in addition the opposing reading lies under the suspicion of ecclesiastical 'normalizing,' the testimony becomes irrefutable. The opposing witnesses represent entirely an ecclesiastical normalizing. That they are in the majority is altogether understandable; if they are ancient, this only proves how early the normalizing process began to operate. For these reasons *ebdomekonta duo* should be printed without square brackets.[9]

I find this conclusion much more satisfactory than Metzger's and so does Howard Marshall who, with commendable brevity says: 'The use of 72 is much less frequent. Hence intrinsic probability strongly favours 72.'[10]

We may therefore take it that there are good grounds for believing that seventy has done duty for the original number seventy-two. This would confirm the legend that the Septuagint, which in Latin is short for *interpretatio septuaginta seniorum* (i.e. the 'translation of the seventy elders'), was in fact the translation of the *seventy-two* elders. As the *Encyclopaedia Judaica* states:

> The Greek version of the Bible known as the Septuagint ... probably owes its name to a story related in the *Letter of Aristeas*, according to which 72 scholars, summoned from Jerusalem by Ptolemy II, Philadelphus (third century BC), achieved a perfect Greek translation of the Pentateuch, which was deposited in the Alexandrian library. This story was embellished with time until the 72 interpreters were credited with the translation of the entire Hebrew Bible. It was maintained that although each of them had worked independently, their finished versions were identical and moreover, superior to the original as a result of divine inspiration.[11]

Other accounts add that the whole of the translation of the seventy-two scholars was completed in 722 days.

I wonder if I am beginning to labour the point? Perhaps; but obviously, if it is one which has been in doubt for so long and is central to my argument, then it is worth spending time attempting to settle it. However, I am now satisfied that I have adduced enough evidence to show that where the number seventy has been used in Luke 10 and possibly in other parts of the Bible, it is probably referring to the number seventy-two. This is very important because if, as E.J. Tinsley indicates, these numbers were symbols 'for something universal,' we are more likely to be able to hazard a guess as to what that universal 'something' was if, for seventy, we can now legitimately read seventy-two.

Why did the number seventy-two symbolize 'something universal' and what was that universal something? Why did Jesus appoint 'a further seventy-two?' Why did the seventy-two come back jubilant? Why not sixty-nine, seventy-five or eighty? Why was it that it was specifically the number seventy-two?

Just as our theory of the Pythagorean Comma in relation to the Hebrew calendar seems to have much more going for it the deeper we look into it, so this same Comma might provide the key to unlock the secrets of the number seventy-two. Is the ratio of the five days to the 360-day year, i.e. 1 to 72, which we established was the approximate ratio of the Comma to the annual cycle, in some way connected with the universal something which the number seventy-two symbolizes in the Bible? Is it more than a coincidence that this Comma ratio, as we have defined it, is 1 to 72?

One day in the Great Year

It could very well be more than a coincidence that seventy-two appears so prominently in the Comma ratio because, if the Comma represents five days in the year, then it would take seventy-two years to make up a complete year of Commas. seventy-two years would thus be equivalent to one year of Pythagorean Commas. Now, as it happens, seventy-two years is a very significant unit of time because it is one degree or one 'day' of what is known variously as the 'Great Year,' the 'Platonic Year,' or the 'Cosmic Year.'

Without going into too much detail, the Great, Platonic, or Cosmic Year is measured by the time it takes for what is called 'the precession of the equinoxes' to complete a cycle. This precession is defined in *Everyman's Encyclopaedia* as: 'A westward movement of the equinoxes on the ecliptic so that they advance to meet the stars and the sun on its annual return.' Its discovery is usually credited to Hipparchus (c.160–120 BC) but, as with many so-called 'Pythagorean' discoveries, it was probably known many centuries earlier.[12] It is caused by 'the pull of the sun and moon, the moon in particular, on the equatorial bulge of the earth. The tendency of the pull is to make the equator coincide with the ecliptic, but the spinning of the earth prevents this and the phenomenon of Precession takes place.'[13] We have spoken about the *axis mundi*, the axle of the world round which the universe was believed to spin. We must now imagine that axis wobbling like a top or an old cartwheel. Giorgio de Santillana and Hertha von Dechend speak about this less well-known dimension of the earth's movement in *Hamlet's Mill*, their great essay on myth and the frame of time:

> Its cause is a bad habit of the axis of our globe, which turns around in the manner of a spinning top its tip being in the centre of our small earth-ball, whence our earth axis, prolonged to the celestial North Pole, describes a circle around the North Pole of the ecliptic, the time 'centre' of the planetary system, the radius of this circle being of the same magnitude as the obliquity of the ecliptic with respect to the equator: $23\frac{1}{2}°$. The time which

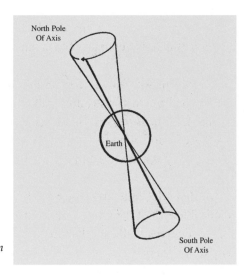

North Pole
Of Axis

Earth

South Pole
Of Axis

Fig.5.1. The precession of the equinoxes.

this prolonged axis needs to circumscribe the ecliptical North Pole is roughly 26,000 years, during which period it points to one star after another: around 3000 BC the Pole Star was alpha Draconis; at the time of the Greeks it was beta Ursa Minoris; for the time being it is alpha Ursa Minoris; in AD 14000 it will be Vega. The equinoxes, the points of intersection of ecliptic and equator, swinging from the spinning axis of the earth, move with the same speed of 26,000 years along with the ecliptic. The Sun's position among the constellations at the vernal equinox was the pointer that indicated the 'hours' of the precessional cycle — very long hours indeed, the equinoxial sun occupying each zodiacal constellation for about 2,200 years.[14]

These details about the astronomy of the Great Year are very complicated for those who know little about this science. It is sufficient for us to be aware in outline of what it is and how long it takes. It is usually computed, as Santillana and Dechend state, at around 26,000 years; but authorities vary as to its precise length. One gives it as 25,765,[15] another as 25,816,[16] another as 25,827[17] and yet another as 25,920. It might seem arbitrary for me to say that I favour the last of these, but I have as good a reason for doing so as for preferring seventy-two to seventy in the earlier discussion. I believe that whatever the precise astronomical length the Great Year was believed to be, it was *taken* as 25,920 years for the sake of musical cosmology which, as we have seen, dominated the thought world of ancient cultures. Ernest McClain explains this in his chapter 'Music and the Calendar:'

> About all we can say for certain about the precessional number 25920 (which is astronomically slightly too large, according to modern measures) is that it fits beautifully into the cosmology of those people who never tried to break the original bonds between music, mathematics and astronomy.[18]

All that McClain says about 25,920 in relation to the exact astronomical length of the Great Year is similar to what we said earlier about the 4.9 degrees of the Pythagorean Comma, in relation to the precise length of the solar year. It is another example of the harmonic number being *taken* to be equivalent to the astronomical one. Elsewhere in his chapter, McClain shows how 25,920 is related to ancient Eastern music and cosmology associated with the Hindu text, the *Rig Veda*. Alain Daniélou also makes this connection in terms which recall Carl Sagan's discussion about Hindu time-cycles in relation to modern theories about the duration of the universe:

> The Pythagorean great year is the fifth part of the Chinese great year of Yuan, equal to $25,920 \times 5 = 129,600$, itself the double of the Hindu manvantara, $25,920 \times 21/2 = 64800$ which, according to Eastern doctrine, always brings humanity back to its starting point. The duration of this complete evolution being two and a half precessions.[19]

It is on the basis of this ancient and apparently universal musical cosmology, as explained by McClain and Daniélou, that I believe we can claim the Great Year was held to be 25,920 years long. If we divide this number by twelve we get a 'month' of 2,160 years (not 2000 as maintained by Dan Brown in *The Da Vinci Code*), and if we divide this month by thirty we get a 'day' of seventy-two years. This unit of seventy-two years is thus one 'day' in the Great Year. I suggest that we may have arrived at last at a reasonable explanation as to why the number seventy-two, and the ecclesiastically normalized number of seventy, should signify 'something universal' in the Bible. It is possible to go even further and say that this unit of seventy-two years was one 'day' in the Cosmic Year because it represented one complete cycle of Pythagorean Commas. We must remember that David Tame speaks in the most far-reaching terms about the Comma's significance:

> The comma is a strange and wide-ranging phenomenon, being literally 'written into' the physical and mathematical laws of the universe. We are entering here into regions of thought difficult for the Western mind to grasp, but the possibility seems to be that it is by the phenomenon of Pythagoras' Comma that the very nature of our lives within the realm of mortality is arranged.[20]

Tame here makes enormous claims for the importance of the Comma and seems to suggest that it may be connected in some way to the very pulse of creation.

Rachaph and the Primal Vibration

Tame speaks at length elsewhere about the physics of vibration and indeed constantly returns to the fundamental link between music, vibration and the created universe. In the section called 'Primal Vibration' he enlarges on his basic contention that the ancients throughout the world believed that 'this Cosmic Vibration was the origin and basis of all matter and energy in the Universe.'[21] In a characteristically arresting paragraph, he links this ancient wisdom with modern science and with various religious traditions:

> And thus we find ourselves throwing light upon the widely-held belief that all matter is composed of one basic substance or energy. According to the great thinkers of old, this energy was Vibration. In modern times, the physical sciences are now arriving back at this original point of departure. Once again, science is beginning to suspect that matter is all composed of one fundamental something, and that the frequencies or rhythms of this something determine the specific nature of each object and atom.
>
> The universal energies were called by the ancient Egyptians the Word of Words of their Gods; to the Pythagoreans of Greece they were the Music of the Spheres; and the ancient Chinese knew them to be the celestial energies of perfect harmony. The Cosmic Tones, as differentiations of the OM, were the most powerful

force in the universe according to the ancients, for these Tones *were* the universe — the very source of the Creation itself.[22]

Impressive though this is, I confess I was surprised that the Egyptians, the Pythagoreans, the Chinese and the Hindus evidently knew all about this primal vibratory force, but not the Hebrews. Although Tame speaks in another chapter, about the biblical concept of the Logos, the Word, I was puzzled that his specific references to *vibration* did not include the Bible. Did its writers not know about it? Did they not even have a word for the basic pulsing energy of the universe?

There is a word in Hebrew which, among other things, can be construed as meaning 'to vibrate.' It is referred to by Gerhard von Rad, a leading Old Testament scholar, in his commentary on Genesis at 1:2: 'and the Spirit of God was moving over the face of the waters.' The word *merachepet* is usually translated 'moved' or 'hovered,' which he says can also be rendered 'vibrate:'

> The much-disputed *merachepet* ... is not to be translated by 'brood,' but according to Deut.32:11 and Jer.23:9, the verb appears to have the meaning of 'vibrate,' 'tremble,' 'move,' 'stir.' This is supported by Dan.7:2, which is to be referred to for interpretation.[23]

This I found most encouraging and was even more surprised to find that another commentator, from a different theological background, went even further than von Rad in this vibratory interpretation. In *Exposition of Genesis*, H.C. Leupold says: 'The verb *rachaph* from which the piel participle is used, *mera(ch)chepheth* signifies a vibrant moving, a protective hovering.'[24] Answering the question — what was the purpose of the Spirit moving over the face of the waters? — he goes on to say:

> We could never believe that this hovering of the Spirit over the face of the waters was idle and purposeless. From all other activities that are elsewhere ascribed to the Holy Spirit we conclude that His work in this case must have been anticipatory of the creative work that followed, a kind of impregnation with divine potentialities. The germs of all that is created were placed into dead matter by Him. His was the preparatory work for leading over from the inorganic to the organic. Koenig in his *Kommentar* feels impelled

to interpret this 'hovering' as 'an intensified and vitalized type of vibration.' We should not be averse to holding that the foundation for all physical laws operative in the world now was laid by this preparatory activity.[25]

If we follow von Rad and Leupold, we are justified in asserting that the Hebrews *did* have their own word for vibration from the root *rachaph*, and that they too can take their place in Tame's list of ancient cultures who knew about the creative power of the primal vibration. In passing, it is worth mentioning how strange it is that Tame has not seen how very similar Genesis 1:2 is to his description of the descent of the Word, as a vibratory force, on the waters of creation. He refers to the Egyptian creation story but could just as well have been describing the biblical 'Spirit of God *vibrating* over the face of the waters,' when he says:

> Only two force principles are at work in everything: matter and dynamic energy. Here, 'matter' equates with the primeval Celestial Waters of the ancient Egyptians. By 'dynamic force' is meant God manifest; meaning the descent of the Word into the Celestial Waters. The descent of this vibratory force gives rise, at its different frequency-levels, to all the supposedly different forms of energy.[26]

This passage reads like a further development of the interpretations of von Rad and Leupold, as if Tame was, like them, a biblical scholar. The likeness is quite remarkable. But what is even more remarkable, and apparently confirmatory of Tame's inadvertent exposition of Genesis 1:2, is the numerical significance of the Hebrew root word *rachaph*. If we analyse the gematria of the three root letters according to the letter-number equivalents as mentioned in Chapter 3, we get r = 200, ch = 8 and ph = 80, so that the total is 288. This number, according to Rabbinic tradition of Chassidic Judaism, represented the 288 sparks into which the Spirit of God divided at the moment of creation on its way into substantiality,[27] but even more significantly for our present study, it will be noticed that 288 is 4 × 72. It is also in an octave relationship to seventy-two because, as demonstrated in the last chapter, octave levels go up and down in multiples and divisions of two. Thus the octave levels from 288 downwards would be

144, 72, 36, 18, 9, etc. This in itself indicates that if we are meant to read a musical significance into the numerology of the word 'vibrate,' seventy-two is in harmonic relation to the pulse of creation. The Pythagorean Comma and one 'day' in the Great Year is thus also written into the Bible as well as into 'the physical and mathematical laws of the universe,' as Tame contends.

The singers and trumpeters in the temple

In *The Myth of Invariance*, it is striking to notice how frequently Ernest McClain refers to the numbers 288 and 72 as octave levels in his section 'Postscript on the Creation of the World.'[28] He analyses the singing in Solomon's temple according to a double octave in which the terminal indices are 288 and 120. These numbers he gets from 1Chronicles 25:7f where, as we discovered in Chapter 4, the number of Levites 'who were trained in singing to the Lord, all who were skilful, was two hundred and eighty-eight' and from 2 Chronicles (5:12) where, as we also found, there were 'a hundred and twenty priests who were trumpeters.' The details of how he works out the notation of this double octave need not concern us except that the octave levels themselves are 288, 144 and 72, with the 288 to 144 being the lower octave. It is perhaps significant that if we imagine that the two rooms of the temple of Solomon represented two octaves, with the lower octave being the Holy Place and the higher octave, the

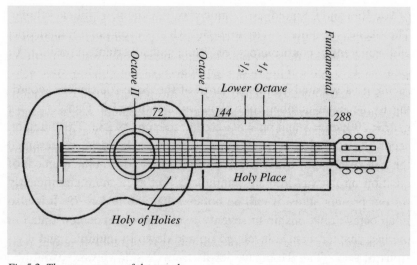

Fig.5.2. The two octaves of the temple.

Holy of Holies, then 288 would be the fundamental note at the entrance wall of the Holy Place and 144 would be the octave higher at the wooden door which divided the two chambers. The number seventy-two would then be the double octave note at the far end wall of the Holy of Holies. These vibrating tones, the primal vibrations that were intoned at the dedication of the temple, may have been the same as those which vibrated in the beginning over the face of the deep. That is to say, the consonances of the universe which, we observed, were built into the proportions of the temple may have been the same as those associated with the Spirit moving, vibrating — i.e. '288-ing' — over the waters at the dawn of creation. If this was so then the 288, 144, 72 double octave might well have been the Hebrew expression of the universal OM, or Cosmic Sound.[29] These may well have been the numbers which represented the overtones of the pulse of the universe.

We saw in Chapter 4 that something very strange happened at the dedication of the temple when the 288 singers and 120 trumpeters raised the song in unison and the whole place was filled with a cloud. We established then that this could be explained by the vibrations of the perfect harmony expressed in the microcosm calling forth the Divine response from the macrocosm. We can now go further and propose that this perfect harmony was vibrating on the overtones of *rachaph*, the Hebrew world for the primal creative sound, associated with the double octave 288, 144 and 72.

This may also give us a new interpretation of the mysterious measurement of the wall of New Jerusalem, where St John says: 'He also measured its wall, a hundred and forty-four cubits by a man's measure, that is, an angel's' (Rev.21:17). If this 144 was meant to be understood as an octave level, then it would be equivalent to the wall of partition between the Holy of Holies and the Holy Place and, like seventy-two, would be harmonically related to 288, the primal pulse of creation. This should not surprise us because the New Jerusalem was, as we have seen, an expanded version of the Holy of Holies. It was the cosmic cube, which contained all the consonances — the primal vibrations — of the universe.

Harmonic 288

In connection with these harmonic numbers of primal vibration, I read a book by Bruce Cathie. On the flyleaf it says of him:

He probes into space-time, throws new light on Einstein's famous $E = MC^2$, and discusses the harmonics of light, sound, temperature, lasers, plant growth and human health. He also shows how scientists, when ready to break out of their present narrow disciplines into the immeasurably wide fields he has thrown open to them, will be able to carry human knowledge to heights undreamed of including life on other planets ... Far-fetched? Too fantastic? The most sceptical reader cannot fail to be impressed by Bruce Cathie's cool and methodical presentation of the facts, and to agree that the harmonic of the speed of light is the key to the understanding of all life and all matter, and to the mysteries of the universe itself.[30]

What did I find was the number of the speed of light according to Bruce Cathie? Why, nothing less than our old friend 144, of course — and without any biblical help! And what is the title of this book? *The Pulse of the Universe*! And its subtitle? *Harmonic 288*! Does Bruce Cathie confirm from his knowledge of the new physics, all that we have deduced from our study of biblical cosmology? Are 72, 144 and 288 related to the pulse beat of the modern, as well as the ancient, understanding of the universe? Is it, after all, 'by the phenomenon of Pythagoras' Comma that the very nature of our lives within the realm of mortality is arranged?'[31] *The Hitchhiker's Guide to the Galaxy* must be wrong! The answer 'to the Ultimate Question of Life, the Universe and Everything'[32] is *not* forty-two as Deep Thought proclaimed, but seventy-two. 'After this the Lord appointed a further seventy-two' — to keep the pulse of his universe.

Is it only a coincidence that the pulse beat of the average adult in good health is seventy-two per minute? And is it, further a coincidence that the numbers of the pentagon-pentagram are five and seventy-two? Perhaps David and Solomon were even wiser than we have so far discovered when they planned and built the pentagonal door into the Holy of Holies, for the numbers five and seventy-two link man with the universe.[33]

6. Great New Year's Day

In the last chapter we established that the most likely meaning of the symbolic number seventy-two in the Bible as a whole and particularly in Jesus' 'Mission of the Seventy-Two,' was that it was a cosmic number, and that as a number of years, it was one 'day' in the Great Year of 25,920 years.

The question I would now like to ask is, are these two references to this number the only indications that New Testament writers were aware that there was such a thing as the Great Year? Even today not many of us know of its existence. Could it be that they were so knowledgeable, where we are so ignorant? Did they really know what the time was on this cosmic clock of the precession of the equinoxes? If you had said to one of them: 'What's the cosmic time, please?' would he have known what you were talking about? In an attempt to answer this, we turn to the New Testament to see if there was any consensus about the times they were living in. Was there any overall consciousness that these were good times, bad times, special or unique times? Was there a general mood, a spirit of the times, an attitude towards their age, epoch or period in history and if so how was it defined?

Not the end of the world but the end of the age

These questions are not hard to answer. Yes, there definitely was a prevalent attitude to the times they were living in. They were times, which were generally thought of as 'the last days,' as many well-known texts demonstrate. For instance, the writer to the Hebrews begins: 'In many and various ways God spoke of old to our fathers by the prophets; but *in these last days* he has spoken to us by a Son.' Sometimes the figure of speech changes from the last days to the last hour as in 1 John (2:18) 'Children, it is *the last hour*; and as you have heard that antichrist is coming, so now many antichrists have come; therefore we know that it is *the last hour*.' These metaphors, which feature the Greek word *eschatos*, meaning 'last,' sometimes change to 'the last times.' Speaking of Christ it says in 1 Peter (1:20): 'He was destined before the foundation of the world but was made manifest *in the last of the times* [*ep'eschatou tôn chronôn*] for your sake.' Although the word for 'times' here is *chronos*, the Jerusalem Bible translates it as 'ages,' saying Christ 'has been revealed only in our time, the end of the ages.'

This free rendering of *chronos* as 'ages,' leads on to other well-known texts associated with the New Testament consciousness of living at the *end* of an epoch. These are those which are connected with the actual word for 'ages,' *aiônôn*. This word, from which we get our word 'aeons.' It is often translated as 'world' in the Authorised Version so that, for instance, the traditional reading of 1 Corinthians (10:11) is 'and they are written for our admonition, upon whom the ends of the world are come.' The Revised Standard Version, which aims at closer adherence to the Greek, corrects this to 'upon whom *the end of the ages* has come.' This Authorised Version translation of *aiôn* as 'world' has been equally misleading in Hebrews (9:26) where it says of Christ: 'But now once in the end of the world hath he appeared to put away sin by the sacrifice of himself.' Once more the word is *aiônôn*, (not *cosmos*, world), a genitive plural, which should read: 'He has appeared once for all *at the end of the ages*.' The Revised Standard Version and the Jerusalem Bible are also not strictly accurate here, putting 'age' in the singular. The New English Bible is too free, speaking about 'at the climax of history.'

This translation of *aiônôn* as 'world' when it should mean 'ages,' has led to the traditional belief that the New Testament writers thought that they were living through not just the end of an age but the end of the *world*. This, together with the frequent rendering of the singular *aiôn* (*age*) also as 'world,' as, for example, in Matthew (28:20): 'And, lo, I am with you alway, even unto the end of the world,' has obscured the fact that in certain texts some of the New Testament writers appear to have been conscious that they were living through a period they characterized not only as 'the last days,' but also, as 'the end of the ages.' I believe that this confusion over the different translations of the words *aiôn* and *aiônôn* has stopped us seeing a link between their consciousness of the times in general, and their specific, though veiled, references to the months of the Great Year, each of which could be described as an age, or aeon. In other words, it has stopped us realizing that when they spoke of the end of the age or series of ages, they were referring to the end of a 'month' or a series of 'months' of the Great Year.

Hermann Sasse's comprehensive analysis of the word *aiôn* in Kittel's *Theological Dictionary of the New Testament*, gives this idea considerable weight.[1] After explaining its different meanings as 'from eternity' and 'to eternity,' 'for ever' and 'never,' especially in John's gospel, 'the eternity of God' and 'the duration of the world,' he then goes on to link it with the theory of eternal recurrence and astrological ages:

> If *aiôn* means the time or duration of the world, and the plural is firmly established, there is an obvious suggestion that the *aiôn* is not unique, but that there is a series of *aiônes* in which all things flow in eternal recurrence. On this view, creation and conclusion are not to be taken in the sense of absolute beginning and end but rather in the sense of transition from one aeon to the other ... This is the doctrine of eternity found in oriental astrology with its thought of eternal recurrence. It can hardly be doubted that this view had some influence on that of the Bible, especially on its eschatological ideas.[2]

This eschatological interpretation of 'age' and 'ages,' being related to astrological epochs, suggests that they may indeed have corresponded to the 'months' of the Great Year. Also, the interpretation of creation and conclusion as not being absolute but relative to the 'transition from one aeon to the other,' confirms my argument.

This evidence from Kittel also allows us to introduce the dimension of cosmic time into our understanding of two more New Testament references which use the Greek words *kairos*, meaning specific time, and *chronos*, meaning time as a whole. These texts are associated with the notion of 'the fullness of time' (*to plerôma tou chronou*, or *tôn kairôn*). The first is Galatians (4:4): 'But when the time had fully come, God sent forth his Son,' and the second is Ephesians (1:10): 'According to his purpose which he set forth in Christ as a plan for the fullness of time, to unite all things in him.' For the first the Jerusalem Bible gives 'but when the appointed time came' and for the second, 'when the times had run their course to the end.' Other translations indicate the same sense that by 'the fullness of time' is meant a specific moment which is both right for Christ to come, and right because a cycle or age of time has been completed and a new one is ready to begin. This concept has a much more positive attitude to the times than those associated with 'the last days' and brings out yet another aspect of New Testament time-consciousness which we can now see in a cosmic dimension. We may say from these texts that there was a belief not only that an age, or series of ages, was ending but that another age was beginning, and that the beginning was associated with the coming of Jesus Christ.

Jesus and the apocalyptic tradition

We noted above that the Authorised Version translation of *aiônôn* and *aiôn*, as 'world' rather than 'ages' or 'age' in certain texts, had given to the New Testament a great sense of impending catastrophe hanging over it, which was not warranted. What a relief to know that for 'end of the world' we can now, in these texts, (as modern translations show) read 'end of the age'! Nevertheless, there was a definite strand of biblical thought which *did* appear to believe that not just the age, but also the world, was about to end. There are a number of passages like 2 Peter (2:8–13) which say in terms suggestive of nuclear war that 'the heavens will be kindled and dissolved, and the elements will melt with fire.' Texts of this type which grip the imagination most are those which report Jesus himself when he speaks of the end being nigh. The most arresting and controversial of these is in Matthew (16:28): 'Truly I say to you, there are some standing here who will not taste death before they see the Son of man coming in his kingdom.' It is sayings such as these which have led many scholars, most notably Albert Schweitzer, to assume that because the end of the world did *not* take place: 'Jesus had after all been mistaken. The Kingdom he expected had never come.'[3] However, difficult though it may be to understand what exactly he *did* mean, most of us, who are outside the fundamentalist camp, would not wish to interpret such texts so literally.

It is in Matthew (24) and related passages in Mark and Luke that we get the most extensive soliloquy on 'the End' in which all the world's future travails are listed: 'And you will hear of wars and rumours of wars; see that you are not alarmed; for this must take place, but *the end* is not yet' (24:6f). If these woes are analysed it appears that Jesus is speaking about two different but complementary types of 'end.' The first is that of the impending destruction of Jerusalem, and is associated with the prophecies that the Roman eagle — 'the desolating sacrilege' — would stand in the holy place (Matt.24:15), that Jerusalem would be surrounded by armies (Luke 21:20), that not one stone of the temple would be left upon another (Matt.24:2), and that the Jews would 'be led captive among all nations' (Luke 21:24). All these things did indeed take place in AD 70. As Albert Nolan comments in *Jesus before Christianity*, 'there can be no doubt that Jesus did prophesy the destruction of Jerusalem by the Romans'[4] and 'What Jesus had to say about the last day was not apocalyptic, it was prophetic.'[5]

The second is that of the literal end of the world as already indicated. In the light of my researches, I propose that Jesus was talking not about the end of the cosmos but about the end of the *age*. It is interesting to consider how many of his eschatological sayings can be explained either as prophecies concerning the imminent collapse of the state of Judea, or as expressions of his awareness of the turmoils that would inevitably accompany the ending of one cosmic age and the beginning of another. Indeed, it is so likely that I propose that these two aspects of the historical process, the national and the cosmic, were the main factors which gave rise to the whole apocalyptic tradition.

Turning to D.S. Russell's *The Jews from Alexander to Herod*, a standard textbook on what is called the Inter-Testamental period, this is precisely what we find. Speaking about the rise of apocalyptic literature from 165 BC, he says that the provision of insights which flourished from that time until the end of the first century AD, 'were inspired by the troublous times in which the Jewish people were then living, first under the Seleucids and then under the Romans.'[6] Regarding our second possible reason for the rise of apocalyptic visions of the End, namely the imminent ending of a cosmic age, or ages, he is equally positive, although he does say that the prophetic phrase 'the latter end of the days,' which had been used to denote the end of an era, 'now indicated not just the end of an historical era, but the end of history itself.'[7] An indiction that by 'era' he means something calculated by the cycles of the heavenly bodies, is given when he is discussing the influence of Zoroastrianism and its teaching that world history could be divided up into four great epochs of three thousand years each, which culminated in a golden age:

> The historical events marking the divisions of history, it is claimed in these writings, are regulated by the movement of the heavenly bodies (cf. *Jub*.4:17,19, etc.) and have been recorded in heavenly tablets cf. *Jub*.1:29, etc.), whose secrets God has now made known to the 'wise' among the people. The impression of 'foretelling' is strengthened by the writers' adoption, as pseudonyms, of the names of ancient worthies — ranging from

Adam to Ezra — to whom the divine secrets, it is said, have been revealed, but which have been kept hidden until now. In this way they are able to relate history in terms of foretelling, and by the calculation of times and seasons to predict the date of the End. Such calculations play a big part in these writings, and make clear not only that the climax of history is at hand but also that there is the closest possible connection between the events of human history and the working out of the divine purpose.[8]

Russell goes on to point out that usually the apocalyptic belief in two ages was characterized by this present evil age, which would pass away and 'the age to come' in which evil would be destroyed forever. This 'age to come' was synonymous with the notion of 'the Kingdom' which would be ushered in as a heaven on earth in which the righteous, victorious over all enemies, would rule with God.

But what is so intriguing from our point of view, is that the understanding of 'two ages' seems to have been fundamental to the apocalyptic tradition and that the exact time of the End, or transition to 'the age to come' was 'regulated by the movement of the heavenly bodies.'[9] Bearing in mind the extent to which we have seen that the New Testament writings were influenced by the apocalyptic tradition, it seems reasonable to suppose that the End-time texts were referring basically to this pervasive 'two age' belief. Furthermore, it is equally reasonable to suppose that the New Testament writers were also aware that numerous attempts to foretell the exact time of the End — or new beginning — were 'regulated by the movement of the heavenly bodies.' With this in mind, we can see a clear connection between our earlier discoveries about the number seventy-two in the Great Year and the 'end of the age' thinking, which is one of the main themes of the New Testament. Is there anything recorded in the life of Jesus that might show us clearly that the New Testament writers saw him specifically as the one who ushered in the end of one age and the beginning of the next? The answer to that must be in the affirmative, because of the likeness which New Testament apocalyptic bears to the Jewish tradition of apocalyptic as a whole. So the next question must be: is there anything recorded in the life of Jesus that indicates that his coming at the end of the age had been predicted exactly 'by the movement of the heavenly bodies?' The answer once again is, yes, there is. In Matthew (2:1–12) we are told about wise men from the East who 'came to Jerusalem, saying "Where is he who has been born king of the Jews? For we have seen his star in the East, and we have come to worship him."' As C.G. Jung says in *Aion*, this story 'proves that Christ, possibly even at the time of the apostles, was viewed from the astrological standpoint.'[10] We must therefore now ask: what was 'his star' and what did it have to do with the end of the age?

The star of Bethlehem

In *The Star of Bethlehem Mystery*, David Hughes begins what must be the most comprehensive and authoritative modern study of this topic by asking the same question:

> What was the star of Bethlehem? Did it really exist? What does it tell us about the birth of Jesus? These questions have been asked throughout the ages and numerous answers have been given over the course of many centuries.[11]

He goes on to list the various celestial phenomena which the star has been thought to be:

> Above all, the star of Bethlehem is a mystery. If it did exist, then it is one of the most amazing phenomena ever witnessed by man. The flow of serious scientific works and popular articles on the star goes on unabated. Theories vary from a nova or supernova to a comet, from a conjunction of Saturn and Jupiter in the constellation of Pisces to Venus, quite apart from other explanations such as a fireball, zodiacal light, ball lightning and the variable star Mira. Even the possibility that the star was simply a legend has to be taken seriously. At the other extreme, an explanation in terms of a miracle beyond the scope of science also has its advocates.[12]

Hughes' book is a brilliant survey of all these possible theories, and it may be a source of some relief to know that we are not going to plod our way through them. Instead, we are going to go straight to his conclusion which, as it happens, turns out to be the interpretation which has been generally held down the centuries, especially since 1603, when the famous astronomer Kepler gave it increased scientific credibility. It is also the interpretation most favoured by contemporary biblical scholars:[13]

> Our conclusion is that the explanation of the star of Bethlehem lies in a tangible physical phenomenon ... the physical occurrence that made up the star of Bethlehem was the series of conjunctions, the apparent coming together in the sky and accompanying risings and settings, of the major planets Jupiter and Saturn. This is not a new conclusion, in fact it can be dated back over seven hundred years, but the movements of Saturn and Jupiter in Pisces fit the large majority of the facts. The Piscean conjunction is rare enough to have been considered unusual. This explanation also has the advantage that the Magi did not have to go continually across the desert for every nova, comet or fireball that happened to appear. It was possible to predict the conjunction, the Babylonian Magi had done just that, as the cuneiform tablets testify. The phenomenon had an inherent astrological message which equated it directly with 'his star' (Matthew 2:2). No comet, nova, fixed star, fireball or whatever could justify this appellation. It was long-lasting, long enough to be seen when the Magi were in their own country, while they were on the journey and on the final leg from Jerusalem to Bethlehem. Historically it occurred at the right time in 7 BC. And finally, even though it was an extremely significant event to a trained astrologer, in reality it consisted of two perfectly normal planets moving as usual along their ordained celestial paths. That is why Herod and the people of Jerusalem could easily miss its significance.[14]

The star then, was no legend or miracle, but an actual astronomical occurrence and an ordinary, if rare, one at that. I have found Hughes' book most convincing and recommend it to all those who wish to follow the discussion in detail. Much the same conclusion is put forward in a popular and shorter account by Werner Keller, in *The Bible as History*.[15] He is most readable and makes the astronomical aspect easy to understand.

So the star of Bethlehem was most probably the series of conjunctions of Jupiter and Saturn in the constellation of Pisces around 7 BC.

Dr Percy Seymour in *The Birth of Christ, Exploding the Myth*, explains succinctly why the Magi thought these particular conjunctions were worth following. They were evidently very rare and symbolically important:

> Jupiter foretold the coming of a king or great leader, Saturn was seen as 'Protector of the Jews' while the constellation of Pisces was associated with the area of Judea. This particular combination of astrological factors made it an extremely rare event which had never taken place before in recorded history. It was the first time that this triple conjunction had occurred in Pisces when the sun was also in Pisces at the point of the vernal equinox.[16]

We will now move on to answer the second part of our question, what did 'his star' have to do with the end of the age as we have come to understand that and the other New Testament phrases relating to the 'End-times?' Hughes himself gives us the first clue towards an answer when he says: 'perhaps the star was ... a sign marking the passage of one age and the dawn of another.'[17] Keller hints even more openly: 'The constellation of Pisces stood at the end of the sun's old course and at the beginning of its new one. What is more likely than that they saw in it the sign of the end of an old age and the start of a new one?'[18]

These comments prompt the question: could it be that, when New Testament writers speak of 'the end of the age,' 'the end of ages,' 'the last days,' 'the fullness of time,' etc., they were really referring to what Hughes calls 'the passage of one age and the dawn of another,' and Keller 'the end of an old age and the start of another?' May we not legitimately connect what Russell has told us, about the general apocalyptic tendency to predict the exact date of the End-time by observations of 'the movement of the heavenly bodies,' with the ancient science and art of astronomy-astrology? Since we have established that Jesus shared the eschatological consciousness of the apocalyptic tradition, should we not therefore link him also with this interpretation?

Giorgio de Santillana and Hertha von Dechend, quoted in the last chapter, have no doubt at all about this. For them the link is clear. The star of Bethlehem did indeed herald a new and blessed age, the age of Pisces:

> But the coming of Pisces was long looked forward to, heralded as a blessed age. It was introduced by the thrice-repeated Great

Conjunction of Saturn and Jupiter in Pisces in the year 6 BC, the star of Bethlehem. Virgil announced the return of the Golden Age under the rule of Saturn, in his famous Fourth Eclogue: 'Now the virgin returns, the reign of Saturn returns, now a new generation descends from heaven on high. Only do thou, pure Lucina, smile on the birth of the child, under whom the iron brood shall first cease, and a golden race spring up throughout the world!' Although promoted to the rank of a 'Christian honoris causa' on account of this poem, Virgil was no 'prophet,' nor was he the only one who expected the return of Kronos-Saturn.[19]

Santillana and von Dechend represent a wide spectrum of scholarship which appears to take for granted that the star of Bethlehem did have a direct relationship to the end of one age and the beginning of another. The age of Pisces was dawning. In another passage they go further and link the star directly with Christ, the Fish, saying 'The advent of Christ the Fish marks our age.'[20]

It would seem, then, from these authorities that what Virgil said in his famous *Fourth Eclogue*[21] was equivalent to what the apocalyptics were predicting as 'the End-time' by observations of 'the movement of the heavenly bodies.' It would thus also appear that we are forging an unexpectedly strong link between the pervasive attitude to 'the last days' in the New Testament and the ages or months of the Great Year.

Santillana and Dechend speak of the new age of Pisces dawning, but some scholars go further and say that a completely new Great Year was starting. In other words that the transition to Pisces was ending one complete cycle of 25,920 years and beginning another. If this was so then no wonder there was turmoil and an increasing belief in the apparent end of the whole world for, as Alan Oken says in *Astrology: Evolution and Revolution*: 'when the Earth progresses into a new World Age, there is a precipitation of incoming energies which causes significant variations in terrestrial occurrences.'[22] Oken is one of those who is convinced that not just a new age but a new Great Year began with Jesus, for he says: 'The transition to the first Age of a new Great Year was personified by the birth of Jesus.'[23] If it was the dawn of not just a new age but a new Great Year then this would, along with all the political portents of doom already mentioned, almost totally explain the pervasive apocalyptic atmosphere which colours the whole of the New Testament writings.

But what precisely *is* a transition from one age to another, or more particularly from one Great Year to another, and how does it link in with the precession of the equinoxes as described in the last chapter? Vera Reid, in her history of the zodiacal ages, *Towards Aquarius*, gives an explanation:

> The transition between the ages of Aries and Pisces marked a turning point both in human evolution and in world history for it coincided with the close of one Great Year and the opening of another ...
>
> The zodiac is composed of twelve glyphs which may be considered as the formula of a sequential life-process applicable to every manifestation of life. Thus man is a microscopic circle whose members and organs reflect the cosmic macrocosm and the twelve divisions of the celestial zodiac. Following the traditional significance of the zodiacal glyphs, Aries, the first sign, governs the head, Taurus the throat and so on round the circle to Pisces, the twelfth sign symbolizing the feet. In the lesser cycle of the common year (365 days) the sun appears to move through the celestial zodiac in order of the signs ... beginning with Aries the head and ending with Pisces the feet. In the 25,000 year cycle of the Great Year, however, the sun, owing to the precession of the equinoxes, appears to move in the reverse direction, that is, from the feet, Pisces, to the head, Aries. Thus, in either case, we may consider that a new cycle comes to birth between these two signs ... In suggesting, therefore, that the Great New Year, or 25,000 year cycle, begins when the sun enters the sign of Pisces we are following the correspondence between the microcosm and the macrocosm.[24]

Thus it would appear from these authorities that we have established a strong case for maintaining that the star of Bethlehem marked not only the end of the age of Aries but also of a complete Great Year, and that it therefore also marked not only the beginning of the age of Pisces, but also of a whole new Great Year.

We now know what our New Testament writer might have answered when we asked him 'What's the cosmic time please?' He surely would have had no hesitation in saying 'Why, it's New Year's Day of course — Great New Year's Day!' According to our calculations, Great New

Year's Day began with the birth of Christ and lasted seventy-two years, until the fall of Jerusalem and destruction of the temple by the Romans. As Jesus foretold, it seemed like 'the last day' and 'the end of the world' for the Jews; but for early Christians, a new heaven and a new earth was being created.

7. Ichthus: the Great Fish

We have now reached something of a turning point in our enquiry. After considering the cosmic significance of the number seventy-two in Chapter 5, we saw in the last chapter that it was no isolated coincidence that this number represented the number of years in one 'day' of the Great Year. We also saw that it was part of a consciousness of 'the End-time,' a consciousness which pervaded the whole New Testament and which, through an examination of the Inter-Testamental apocalyptic tradition, we were able to link with the end, not only of a cosmic age or 'month' but also of a complete Great Year. We saw too, in the star of Bethlehem, a very clear connection between the Great Year and the birth of Jesus Christ.

I want next to follow the star a little further, to see if we can discern any consciousness in the New Testament that the age of Aries was ending and that the age of Pisces was beginning. In other words, just as in the last chapter we considered the general New Testament attitude to 'the times,' so now I want to ask: are there any texts within the New Testament which suggest that there might have been an awareness that it was specifically the age of *Aries* that was ending and the age of *Pisces* beginning? Possible texts immediately spring to mind when we remember that Aries means Ram and Pisces means Fish.

The ram-lamb

C.H. Dodd, in his authoritative work *The Interpretation of the Fourth Gospel*, considers that in the New Testament the words *amnos* and *arnion* (translated as *lamb*) can also allude to a young horned ram. He holds that these Greek words appear to have been adopted by some Greek-speaking Christians as images of the Messiah — 'the leader of the flock of God' — as well as images of the Passover sacrificial victim. He maintains that when John the Baptist said 'Behold the Lamb of God who takes away the sin of the world' (John 1:29) he meant 'God's messiah who makes an end of sin.'[1] This famous Johannine text is, of course, just one of several in the New Testament which we have come to associate principally with the central doctrine of Christ's vicarious suffering on our behalf (cf. Acts 8:32; 1Cor.5:7; 1Pet.1:19).

It is, however, by no means easy to demonstrate that the symbol of the Lamb in the New Testament had any astrological significance. It is all very well to imply, because the Messiah's death as sacrificial Lamb of God coincided with the end of the age of Aries, that the New Testament writers were aware, as Kenneth Cuming asserts in *God and the New Age*, that Christ had 'brought to an end the Age of Aries the Ram by becoming the living symbol in Himself.'[2] But what justification have we got for this inference? Just because the whole concept of the lamb of sacrifice coincided with the Arian age, it does not necessarily mean that this was more than a coincidence. Similarly just because the sacrifice of lambs did in fact end a generation after Jesus died, when the temple was destroyed, it does not necessarily follow that these events were in any way connected.

The fish

It is equally hard to prove, just because there are twenty-eight passages in the gospels which refer to fish, that they necessarily indicate that the writers wished to tell us in sign language that the Piscean age had begun. After all, it is reasonable to assume that disciples who were selected from villages around the Sea of Galilee, would have had more than a passing interest in the fish trade, even if not all of them were themselves fishermen; and that this alone could account for many, if not all, of the 'fish' texts in the gospels. What cosmic significance, for instance, can we with any credibility extrapolate from Luke 24:24 where we are told that when the resurrected Jesus asked his disciples 'Have you anything here to eat?' they 'gave him a piece of broiled fish, and he took and ate before them?' It seems ludicrous to imply from this that they gave Jesus a piece of broiled fish because he was the great Fisherman of the new Piscean age! It was as natural for them to happen to have some fish on the broil as for us to heat up something out of the freezer.

Yet having said this, and after making all due allowances for the scepticism which naturally arises in minds which have been taught by the Church[3] and by science[4] to be dismissive of all astrological inferences, there is another area of evidence to which we should now turn. This is an area which is not so easy to dismiss, which does imply that the New Testament writers were most probably well aware of the link between the fish and Pisces. I refer to the symbolism of the Early Church.

Ichthus in the Early Church

The Christian symbol of the fish first appeared in Alexandria around AD 200, and William Neil, in *The Christian Faith in Art*, says that thereafter it became so important that it was recognized as *the* Christian sign, summing up all the important doctrines of the faith:

> The sacramental symbols of Baptism as the beginning of the new life of the Christian, and of the Eucharist as a dramatization of the Passion and Resurrection, are summed up by the quasi-Biblical imagery of the Fish which features so largely in early Christian painting. The letters of the Greek word for fish, *ichthus*, were ingeniously seen to be the initial letters of the Greek Words 'Jesus Christ, Son of God, Saviour' and to the Christians of the second century no symbol said so much. It stood for Incarnation, Redemption, Resurrection — the whole scheme of Christian salvation.[5]

After listing all these profound and comprehensive meanings of the symbol of the fish, in the next sentence Neil goes on to say that the fish became so important because 'it was historically linked with the miracle of the Loaves and Fishes and the apostolic vocation to become "fishers of men".'[6] At first glance these two biblical references would seem to give sufficient reason for the central importance of the fish to second-century Christians. But are they really? Are these and the other fishy texts enough to have made this sign become *the* expression of 'Incarnation, Redemption, Resurrection — the whole scheme of Christian salvation?' I don't think so. I believe there would have to have been an even more profound meaning for this sign to have virtually taken over the faith and become *the* icon of the Early Church. This deeper, universal meaning from which all the other references took their added significance, I believe, could only have been that of the Piscean age.

Gilbert Cope, in the chapter 'Early Christian Art' in *Symbolism in the Bible and in the Church*, has a section which amplifies Neil. He lists the different meanings of the fish symbol:

> In early Christian art a Fish, in the first place, signifies the soul of the departed; secondly it signifies the eucharistic spiritual

food; thirdly it signifies the presence of Christ himself, for very early it had been noticed that the letters of the Greek word for fish — I-Ch-Th-U-S — acrostically provided the initials for Jesus-Christ-of God-Son-Saviour. The Fish, in the early Christian centuries, was therefore a very powerful symbol indeed.[7]

Like Neil, Cope explains the importance of the fish by referring to the variety of New Testament texts:

In the Gospels there is a great deal about boats and fishing: several of the disciples were fishermen, Jesus travelled in and preached from a boat, he stilled a storm and walked on water, he spoke of 'fishers of men,' he referred to Jonah in the whale's belly as a type of his resurrection (Matthew 12:39f) and to Noah's flood as a type of his *eschaton* (Luke 17:26–30), fishes were eaten at the eucharistic meals when the crowds were fed, there was a coin in a fish's mouth, after the seven disciples had caught 153 the Risen Lord gave them fish and bread to eat (John 21:1f).[8]

But are these texts enough to account for the sustained ascendancy of the fish over other symbols such as the lamb or the light? Edward Hulme is one who does not think so. In *Symbolism in Christian Art*, he finds it inexplicable and objectionable:

It is somewhat curious that such a symbol (the fish) should have held its ground so long, since it sprang merely from a verbal or rather a literal coincidence, and that too of a somewhat forced nature. It had nothing of the poetical feeling of that beautiful symbol, the Lamb, not did it express like the lion, anything of the royal majesty of the great King of kings. The form was based on no allusion in any text, and the difference and distance between the cold-blooded and apathetic creature of the waters and the Creator, the Lord of all, who suffered so freely for the sheep of His pasture, is something infinitely great, and would, we should have thought, have led men earlier to feel how unworthy the symbol was of One so infinitely tender, One so immeasurably exalted.[9]

Hulme's sentiments are, I believe, thoroughly understandable. The 'cold-blooded and apathetic creature of the waters' symbolizing the infinitely tender and exalted Saviour. How inappropriate! What have they got in common? Surely nothing at all. I am so sympathetic to this position that I suggest that the whole thing *is* inexplicable unless we see in it the underlying reference to the Piscean age. After all, why should it interest the early Church quite so much that the Greek word for fish spelt out the initials of Jesus-Christ-Son of God-Saviour? So what? Surely Hulme is right when he says that this is merely a 'verbal, or rather literal coincidence, and that too of a somewhat forced nature.' For nowhere in the New Testament is Jesus himself ever referred to as the Fish. The lamb, the light of the world, the bread of life, the door of the sheep etc., yes, — but never the Fish. How else can we explain that not only did the fish become *the* symbol of the faith for the Early Church but also actually symbolized the person of Jesus himself? *Ichthus* symbolized Jesus Christ, not just the sum of Christian doctrine, and this was evidently the case as much for the Early Church Fathers as for the iconographers.

Writing in the third century, Tertullian says: 'we little fishes, following the example of our Fish Jesus Christ, are born in water.'[10] A third-century Christian tombstone at Autun states 'Divine offspring of the heavenly Fish ...'[11] and Bishop Abercius of Hieropolis around AD 200, speaking of the eucharistic bread, said 'set before me for food the Fish ... whom a spotless Virgin caught.'[12] These and other early Christian writers saw Christ himself as the Fish. The Fish for them had supplanted all other New Testament images as a symbol of all doctrine *and* of Jesus himself. I must confess that I cannot see any justification for the dominance of this image over the other legitimate New Testament metaphors other than the pervasive consciousness that Christ's birth had ushered in the new age of Pisces, and that the new spiritual energies associated with him were somehow also associated with a specifically Piscean spirituality. This is the opinion of Herbert Whone in *Church, Monastery, Cathedral*. Under the paragraph *Fish*, he writes:

> The fish as a symbol is closely connected with Christ. In the early Church he was called Iesous Ichthus (Jesus the Fish) or sometimes 'the Great Fish.' This was because Christ's birth heralded the beginning of the zodiacal era of 2150 years, the Sign of Pisces (The Fishes).[13]

Whone then goes on to speak about a specifically Piscean spirituality:

> The Piscean Era has much to do with the washing away of impurity, with renunciation and suffering, in order to make way for the new cycle of spiritual awareness, the Age of Aquarius. In terms of the individual, the image of the fish suggests the material and psychic sea in which a man flounders. But it is Christ, descending into this sea, embracing all men in an act of sacrificial redemption, that shows the opposite face of Pisces. And man's confusion in the sea is redeemed by his own developing capacity for love and compassion.[14]

It seems, then, that an examination of the New Testament texts, which refer to fish, does not in itself justify us in our coming to the conclusion that they had any explicit astrological significance. However, now that we have looked into the evidence of the Early Church, it does appear that we would be justified in agreeing with Herbert Whone. We can corroborate his position from the conclusion we came to in the last chapter regarding the apocalyptic tradition and the star of Bethlehem. We accepted that 'his star' was most probably the series of conjunctions of Jupiter and Saturn in the constellation of Pisces. We can now understand that the new ascendancy of the constellation of Pisces would be the most likely reason why the followers of Jesus pictured him as the Great Fish even though he was not so designated in the New Testament. We can now also understand that, as Whone points out, the qualities we associate with him, i.e. washing away of impurity, renunciation, suffering and compassion, were specifically Piscean attributes, and that, therefore, the fish would also inevitably come to be seen as a symbol of 'Incarnation, Redemption, Resurrection — the whole scheme of Christian salvation.'

Indeed, I think we can, on the principle of 'as above, so below,' go so far as to accept the increased influence of the constellation of Pisces as the most likely explanation of why the symbol of the fish gained such an ascendancy within Christianity in the centuries after the New Testament canon was closed. Consequently, we should now have serious reservations about agreeing with Edward Hulme that it is 'somewhat curious that such a symbol should have held its ground so long.'

The vesica piscis in sacred geometry

There is another department of traditional symbolism, which has always assumed a fundamental connection between Jesus Christ and the Piscean age. This is the ancient art-science of sacred geometry, which we encountered in relation to the New Jerusalem and Solomon's temple. The specific geometrical figure to which both Christ and the fish are related is what is known as the *vesica piscis*, the vessel or bladder of the fish. This is the lozenge or almond shape formed by two interpenetrating circles whose centres lie on each other's circumference.

Herbert Whone explains the profound significance of this simple figure, which is also known as the mandorla, the Italian word for almond:

> The mandorla is the almond-shaped line drawn around the full-length figure of Christ, usually with fine lines radiating outwards from the body, showing the perfected inner light of divinity ... The mandorla is associated with Christ in majesty, though later, in medieval times, it became common to depict the Virgin Mary in the same way. Another name for it is the 'mystic almond.'
>
> The image of the almond is a reference to the fruit of the tree which by its form suggests the womb, thus the womb of the world from which all developed and within which the redemptive power of Christ operates. The almond tree is itself associated with purity of birth ...
>
> The mandorla is also known as the *vesica piscis* (Latin, 'bladder of the fish'), again an image of the waters of the womb of the

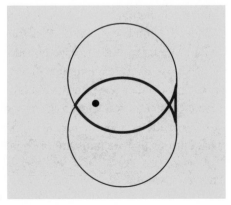

Fig.7.1. The vesica piscis.

world within which the Christ power radiates. In this sense Christ is the 'Great Fish' in the sea, having descended into that sea to redeem floundering humanity. Sometimes the mandorla is referred to as an *ichthus*, Greek 'fish,' and again simply as the 'aureole.' It is exclusively the property of Christ and the Virgin.[15]

Whone here brings together the complementary meanings of the *vesica piscis*, i.e. the bladder of the fish, the mandorla and the almond. It is surprising to find ourselves back to the fruit of the almond tree, which, as we discovered in our examination of the seven-branch candlesticks in the temple, was the tree of life for the Hebrews. Perhaps it was given this pre-eminence as much for its womb-shaped fruit and importance in sacred geometry as for its beautiful early blossom. Whether this was the case or not, it is obvious that the almond shape does look like a womb and that this association was more than metaphorical. For just as Whone says it suggested 'the womb of the world from which all developed,' so according to John Michell, it is a geometrical fact that it is 'the

Fig.7.2. Christ within the vesica.

womb from which are generated all the numbers and ratios of the Temple.'[16]

Robert Lawlor agrees, saying: 'The Vesica is also a form-generator in that all the regular polygons can be said to arise from the succession of vesica constructions.'[17]

Is it once more fortuitous or, as Edward Hulme might say, 'a literal coincidence, and that too of a somewhat forced nature,' that the womb-like shape, the geometric importance, the association with Christ and the Piscean age all come together in this figure? Is it also a coincidence that from early in the Piscean age, the bishop's mitre 'assumed the shape of a fish-head with reference to Christ who was known to the early Christians as the Great Fish?'[18]

Whone, Michell and Lawlor do not think so. Lawlor is particularly explicit about the link between the *vesica*, Christ and the age of Pisces:

> The overlapping circles — an excellent representation of a cell, or any unity in the midst of becoming dual — form a fish-shaped central area which is one source of the symbolic reference to Christ as a fish. Christ, as universal function, is symbolically this region which joins together heaven and earth, above and below, creator and creation. The fish is also the symbolic designation of the Piscean Age, and consequently the Vesica is the dominant geometrical figure for this period of cosmic and human evolution, and is the major thematic source for the cosmic temples of this age in the west, the Gothic cathedral. Jesus as the centre of the Vesica carries the idea of the non-substantial, universal 'Christic' principle entering into the manifest world of duality and form. The Piscean Age has been characterized as that of the formal embodiment of spirit, manifesting a deeper penetration of spirit into form, with a concurrent deepening of the materialization of spirit: the Word becomes flesh.[19]

Enough has now been said in this and the previous chapter to substantiate the proposition that in the New Testament writings implicitly and in the Early Church explicitly, there was a pervasive consciousness that Jesus Christ was not only the Saviour from sin, the Redeemer of the individual soul, but that he was also the embodiment of a specifically Piscean spirituality. There would appear to be sufficient evidence to maintain that there was a widespread realization that a new age had begun in and through him and that the eternal Word which had become flesh had done so as *ichthus*, the Great Fish.

We are at last, I believe, coming to a position from which we can begin to look at the Bible and some traditional Christian presuppositions from a new perspective. This is the perspective of the Great Year, each age or 'month' of which as we have seen is approximately 2160 years long. Once we learn to view the panorama of the ages rising and falling according to these 'months,' then a new way of relating our faith and the Bible to the historical process opens up to us. We can begin to chart our own position in relation to this process and begin also to understand precisely *why* the millenarian literalists mentioned in the introduction, have got it wrong. For just as the traditional interpretation of New Testament apocalyptic mistook the end of the *age* for the end of *world*, so today many who espouse Armageddon theology are doing the same. Indeed the very fact that so many are doing so, at least in America, may itself be a sign of the approaching end of the age, of new-age consciousness.

We have now established beyond any reasonable doubt that the writers of the New Testament believed Jesus Christ had universal and cosmic significance. Understanding this can help us interpret the signs of *our* times and find hope for *our* future. It is in the context of the ages of the Great Year that I believe this can be done, for it is not the world which is going to end soon but it is the age — the age of Pisces. There are great changes taking place because, as Alan Oken has told us, 'When the Earth progresses into a new World Age, there is a precipitation of incoming energies which causes significant variations in terrestrial occurrences.' If you were asked 'What's the cosmic time, please?' what would you answer? Did you know that, according to the precession of the equinoxes, the age of Pisces will soon be ending, and that this is the dawning of the age of Aquarius?

8. Aquarius: the Spirit Pourer

We now come to a consideration of the Age of Aquarius which, according to many accounts, is dawning in our time. As the famous song from *Hair* asserted so emphatically, 'This is the dawning of the Age of Aquarius.' In Chapter 7 we looked for New Testament texts and Early Church symbols, which showed that there was a general awareness that the Age of Pisces had begun. Now, we are going to look for evidence of Aquarian symbolism. After all, if it really is the beginning, or nearly the beginning of a new age, then there should be something about it — and indeed about all future ages — pre-figured in the New Testament. It would be a terrible thing if we had to go into the Aquarian age still clutching our old Piscean symbols.

The man carrying a jar of water

At first it would seem a tall order. Aquarian symbolism in the Bible seems an unlikely proposition. Remembering that Aquarius is the Water Carrier we could, of course, ask ourselves whether we can think of any text in the gospels which refers to a water-carrier. One obvious one comes to mind: Mark 14:13 (cf. Luke 22:10) where Jesus, in the course of giving his disciples instructions regarding the preparations for the Last Supper, said:

> Go into the city, and a man carrying a jar of water will meet you; follow him, and wherever he enters, say to the householder, 'The teacher says: Where is my guest room, where am I to eat the passover with my disciples?' And he will show you a large upper room furnished and ready; there prepare for us.

This story is a favourite one among astrologers hunting for Aquarian texts.[1] It is referred to as the foreshadowing of the age after Pisces by Peter Lemesurier, in *Gospel of the Stars*, who sees the whole of the Last Supper as symbolic of the millennial banquet:

Fig.8.1. Aquarius as water pourer.

... the pilgrims of humanity will be met by a man carrying a pitcher of water. Not the woman whose normal task it was. But a man. A man thereby identifies himself.

As Aquarius.

And as the celestial water-carrier comes to meet them, they in turn must follow him. To an upper room. A large upper room, already prepared.

'I go to prepare a place for you,' said Jesus. 'And if I go and prepare a place for you, I shall come again and receive you to myself, so that where I am you may be also.'

And now, in symbol, that moment had come.

For there, in that large upper room which represents the limitless higher planes, the exalted dimensions of the coming Millennium, a feast had been prepared. The Passover-supper, the Messianic Banquet which throughout the prophecies had never ceased to symbolize the future Golden Age ...[2]

I do not doubt that this 'man carrying a jar of water' could possibly be a symbol of Aquarius. Nor do I doubt that once you have made up your mind that he *is* Aquarius, the upper room may well become symbolic of the millennial banquet. Nevertheless, the overall impression I am left with is that Lemesurier's imagination is a little too lively and that his symbolic interpretation has gone a bit over the top. It is too easy to turn the gospel stories into allegories and I would need more than this one man carrying a water jar in order to be convinced that Aquarius is in the New Testament. It is not that I think Lemesurier and those who follow this interpretation are necessarily wrong. It is just that they make too much of it. I am not convinced that this text *is* the main one we are looking for. After all, there were twenty-eight texts, which spoke about fish for the Piscean age. Surely there ought to be more than one, which speaks about water-carriers for the Aquarian. Where can they be found?

The out-pouring of the Spirit

Looking at pictorial representations of Aquarius, you will notice two things, which I believe are important in the quest for possible Aquarian texts. The first is that the Water Carrier is usually pictured *pouring* his water out, never just *carrying* it. He is seldom drawn as 'a man carrying a jar of water,' but very often as a man pouring a jar of water. He is not so much a water carrier as a water pourer. The second is that he is always pictured as being up in the air, pouring his water down onto the earth. When we also realize that, according to Vera Reid, the water which he is pouring 'is not the water of the earth' but 'the Water of Life,'[3] we are ready to redefine our question: can we think of any New Testament texts which speak about the Water of Life being poured out from the sky onto the earth? Well, there is one which leaps to mind if by 'Water of Life' is meant something like the Spirit. This is the famous one from the prophet Joel, quoted by Peter (Acts 2:17f) to justify the strange phenomena of speaking in tongues, which had just broken out amongst the disciples on the day of Pentecost, ten days after Jesus' ascension and fifty after his resurrection, when he said:

> But this is what was spoken by the prophet Joel:
>> 'And in the last days it shall be, God declares,
>> that I will pour out my Spirit upon all flesh,
>> and your sons and daughters shall prophesy,
>> and your young men shall see visions,

and your old men shall dream dreams;
yea, and on my menservants and my maidservants
   in those days
I will pour out my Spirit; and they shall prophesy.'

The expression 'I will pour out,' is only a figure of speech in Joel's prophecy and is used in several other contexts in the New Testament.[4] Nevertheless it seems to have been integral to the way in which the disciples described their experience of the Spirit at Pentecost. Luke refers to it again in exactly the same way in Acts 2:33 and 10:45. Speaking of the Gentile Pentecost, which came later, he said 'the gift of the Holy Spirit had been poured out even on the Gentiles.'

Unlike the 'man carrying the jar of water,' these two texts are of supreme importance in the New Testament because they describe the first Pentecost, which is usually thought of as the birthday of the Jewish Church, and the second 'Pentecost,' which began the Gentile Church. In both, the image used of the Spirit is that it was 'poured out.'[5] The 'man carrying a jar of water' led the disciples to the upper room but disappeared into the shadows without a word, still *carrying* his jar of earthly water. But at Pentecost the waters of life were not merely carried across the stage of history, they were actually poured out. I believe it is these two texts, which may be legitimately taken to be symbolic of Aquarius, because of their metaphorical appropriateness and central importance. This is further borne out if we look more closely at the story of Pentecost.

The baptism in the Holy Spirit

This pouring out of the Spirit at Pentecost is also called the 'baptism in the Holy Spirit.' Just before his ascension Jesus told his disciples not to depart from Jerusalem, but to wait for the promise of the Father, which, he said 'you heard from me, for John baptized with water, but before many days you shall be baptized with the Holy Spirit' (Acts 1:4f). Jesus' reference to John the Baptist drew the distinction between his own baptism in the Holy Spirit and John's baptism in water. This occurred at the beginning of his ministry, at the time when John had testified in these terms: 'I saw the Spirit descend as a dove from heaven, and it remained on him. I myself did not know him; but he who sent me to baptize with water said to me, "He on whom you see the Spirit descend and remain, this is he who baptizes with the Holy Spirit".' (John 1:32). This text is recorded in all four gospels; Matthew and Luke add that Jesus would baptize 'with the Holy Spirit *and with fire.*'

It is an extraordinary fact that throughout the Christian era, apart from the reference to 'he breathed on them, and said to them "Receive the Holy Spirit"' (John 20:22), at Anglican and Catholic Confirmation services, this baptism with the Holy Spirit has gone largely unnoticed. It hardly features at all as a distinctive doctrine or article of faith. By contrast, however, baptism in water has not only featured prominently, but has also been the subject of bitter and heated theological controversy — and still is. The Catholics and the Anglo-Catholics, for instance believe in what is known as baptismal regeneration, i.e. that the action of baptizing by sprinkling the head with water actually confers the grace of salvation, the washing away of sins through the blood of Christ. The Baptists on the other hand are a distinctive denomination largely because they believe in baptism for believers only by total immersion. To be a Christian in almost any denomination means making up your mind not on *whether*, but on *how*, important water baptism is, whereas baptism in the Holy Spirit is scarcely ever mentioned.

If baptism in the Holy Spirit is so important in the New Testament, how is it that it has been neglected throughout Church history? If John the Baptist implied that his water baptism for the remission of sins was as nothing compared to Jesus' Spirit baptism, how can we explain that the churches have been so totally taken up with the former but not with the latter? Could the answer possibly be that throughout the Piscean age anything to do with the symbolism of water took precedence over anything to do with air? Fish swim in water. Pisces is a water sign. Fish will only take air through water, never through the air or they die — like fish out of water. By contrast Aquarius is an air sign. He lives up in the air and the 'water' he pours out is the airy world of the Spirit. It should follow then that if we are moving towards the Aquarian age, and if our New Testament 'Aquarian' textual interpretations are on the right lines, we might expect Spirit baptism to be becoming more important and water baptism less so. Strangely enough, while it might be difficult to substantiate the latter, the former is most definitely the case, as anyone who has had dealings with the Pentecostal and Charismatic movements knows.

The Pentecostals and Charismatics

It is a startling fact of ecclesiastical life today that all over the world Christians are having the experience of what they call the 'baptism in the Holy Spirit' as on the first day of Pentecost. The Pentecostal Churches number millions and so now do the Charismatics, that is to say, the Pentecostals *within* the historic denominations. It is a remarkable phenomenon, and it is a twenty-first century one. At a time when we speak of the 'post-Christian age' and the 'secular world,' the Pentecostals, since their beginnings in 1900, have consistently experienced an exponential rate of growth.[6] How can we understand this when many other churches are in decline? Could it be that, as the Piscean Age wanes and the Aquarian Age begins, so Christ is manifesting himself in his new role as Aquarius the Spirit Pourer who, 'baptizes in the Holy Spirit?' Not that he wasn't always this from the first Pentecost, but it is only now 'in the fullness of time' that this particular aspect of his person and work can be received.

In the light of what has been said earlier about the numbers seventy and seventy-two, it is notable that seventy years before the Pentecostal movement began, there was a mini-Pentecost, which pre-figured the twentieth-century out-pouring in almost every respect. This was the revival in the early 1830s in the west of Scotland and London, associated with the name of Edward Irving, which developed into the denomination known as the Catholic Apostolic Church.[7]

Irving was a famous preacher in London and was the first theologian since Tertullian in the early third century to speak and write about the baptism in the Holy Spirit as a distinctive doctrine.[8] He wrote a tract called *The Day of Pentecost, or the Baptism with the Holy Ghost*, in which he taught that the experience of Pentecost was the birthright of every believer.[9] Why did so many centuries have to pass before such an obvious and central doctrine could be rediscovered and proclaimed? This was something he wondered about himself:

But what then are we to make of our fathers, who knew little or nothing of this [the baptism in the Holy Spirit], and had no marks of possessing it; not the Reformers; nor the saints and martyrs later than the third century? I have given thee rest on this question. They might still have regeneration and remission, and the grace of both sacraments: but God is leading us of this age back to fountains of which our fathers never drank; which were open to them indeed, as to the first Christians, but the way unto them was not known.[10]

Why was it that the way back to these living fountains was only discovered in 1830? Could it be that the God who 'is leading us of this age back to fountains of which our fathers never drank' was the God and Father, not only of the Great Fish, but of the Water Carrier, the Spirit Pourer? After all, 1830 years out of the allotted 2160 years of the age of the Great Fish had passed. 1830 stood at 25.5 degrees to 30 degrees of Pisces. Over $^5/_6$ of the Piscean 'month' had gone. All across the nation, there was a new vibration. New awarenesses were emerging. New symbols were assuming power. Old ones were becoming superannuated. Perhaps it was more than a coincidence that almost exactly one 'day' later in the Piscean 'month' in 1900, the Spirit Pourer began to manifest himself in that way again.

If Edward Irving may thus be regarded as the forerunner of this particular understanding of Aquarian spirituality, then his close friend and fellow native of Annandale, Dumfriesshire in Scotland, Thomas Carlyle, may perhaps be thought of as the precursor of those who have since made comparative studies of the rise and fall of religious myths and symbols, such as Sir James Frazer in *The Golden Bough*, Carl Jung in *Aion*, Joseph Campbell in *The Masks of God* and Erich Neumann in *The Great Mother*. Published in 1835, the year after Irving's untimely death, *Sartor Resartus* (literally 'the tailor patched') is a witty and profound parable about the superannuation of symbols seen in the metaphor of clothes that wear out, as W.H. Hudson points out in the introduction to the *Everyman's Library* edition:

> All dogmas, forms and ceremonials, he teaches, are but religious vestments — symbols expressing man's deepest sense of the divine mystery of the universe and the hunger and thirst of the soul for God. It is in response to the imperative necessities of his nature that he moulds for himself these outward emblems of his ideas and aspirations. Yet they are only emblems; and since, like all other human things, they partake of the ignorance and weakness of the times in which they were framed, it is inevitable that with the growth of knowledge and the expansion of thought they must presently be outgrown. When this happens, there follows what

Carlyle calls the 'superannuation of symbols.' Men wake up to the fact that the creeds and formulas which have come down to them from the past are no longer living for them, no longer what they need for the embodiment of their spiritual life.[11]

There are many passages of *Sartor Resartus* which could be quoted as examples of this, but from our point of view, one about the Church is very apposite because it speaks not only of the present 'out-at-elbows' clothes, but also of the future 'new vestures' which are being secretly woven:

Meanwhile, in our era of the World, those same Church-Clothes have gone sorrowfully out-at-elbows; nay far worse, many of them have become mere hollow Shapes or Masks, under which no living Figure or Spirit any longer dwells; but only spiders and unclean beetles, in horrid accumulation, drive their trade; and the mask still glares on you with its glass-eyes, in ghastly affectation of Life — some generation-and-half after Religion has quite withdrawn from it, and in unnoticed nooks is weaving for herself new Vestures, wherewith to reappear, and bless us, or our sons or grandsons.[12]

Although Carlyle does not tell us exactly what symbols have become superannuated and what are the new 'masks of God,' all that he says in terms of those 'clothes' which are either 'out-at-elbows' or being secretly woven into 'new Vestures,' runs parallel to Irving's God who is 'leading us of this age back to fountains of which our fathers never drank.' It also fits the basic astrological belief that, as Liz Greene puts it in *Relating*:

At the close of an era, many old gods die or are subordinated, and new gods — gods who are symbolic of energies which have not emerged into human consciousness before — are born[13] ... What man worships as the highest possible ideal, the highest good and the highest mystery behind life, appears to be in some way symbolized by the governing astrological sign, and this mystery always embodies something entirely new, something previously unknown to man's consciousness.[14]

There is another aspect of *Sartor Resartus* in which Carlyle parallels Irving and in which he may perhaps be seen as an Aquarian prophet. This is in his experience of 'conversion' in the *Rue Saint-Thomas del'Enfer.* In the guise of his hero, Diogenes Teufelsdröckh, Carlyle describes how one day he confronted all his despair and fears and defied them, with astonishing effect:

> Thus had the EVERLASTING NO (*das ewige Nein*) pealed authoritatively through all the recesses of my Being, of my ME; and then it was that my whole ME stood up, in native God-created majesty, and with emphasis recorded its Protest. Such a Protest, the most important transaction in Life, may that same Indignation and Defiance, in a psychological point of view, be fitly called. The Everlasting No had said: 'Behold, thou are fatherless, outcast, and the Universe is mine' (the Devil's); to which my whole Me now made answer: 'I am not thine, but Free, and forever hate thee!'
>
> It is from this hour that I incline to date my Spiritual New-Birth, or Baphometic Fire-Baptism; perhaps I directly thereupon began to be a Man.[15]

What is important to notice in this famous account of how the 'Everlasting No' began to change into the 'Everlasting Yea,' is the symbolism of baptism which Carlyle uses to describe it. We may take the word 'Baphometic' to mean no more than 'mysterious,' since it is derived from a mythical androgynous icon, the Baphomet.[16] But fire baptism is not such an arcane concept since it comes directly from Matthew (3:11) and Luke (3:16), quoted above: 'he will baptize you with the Holy Spirit *and with fire.*' So even the doubting Thomas, while rejecting the out-at-elbows Calvinism of his parents, could not stop himself describing this 'most important transaction in Life' in terms of baptism — not the water baptism of the Church but the fire baptism which is so closely linked to the Spirit baptism that most commentators take it to be part of the same thing.[17] Obviously it would have been inappropriate for him to have used a phrase which had a well-known Christian meaning. Why then should he have called it a 'Fire-baptism?' And why, for that matter, should Matthew and Luke have added 'and with fire?' It is usually assumed that the answer to the latter lies in its association with the spiritual winnowing that would involve the chaff being burned 'with unquenchable fire' (Matt.3:12; Luke 3:17).[18] While this is undoubtedly the case, it may also perhaps, in the context of our present study, be taken to represent Leo, the polar opposite, or complementary sign, of Aquarius. Although this may sound unlikely at first, we must remember that in astrological theory, it is held that the signs of the zodiac come in pairs of opposites. Thus the Age of Pisces, to be more correct, is the Age of Pisces-Virgo since Virgo, the Virgin, is the complementary sign of the Fish. Virgo is an earth-sign whose attributes balance those of the watery Pisces. Likewise, to be completely accurate, we should be speaking not just about the Age of Aquarius, but of Aquarius-Leo. Leo is a fire sign whose qualities complement those of airy Aquarius. Thus along these lines we could see the Irvingite, Pentecostal and Carlylean interpretation of 'he will baptize you with the Holy Spirit and with fire' as symbolizing the change from the water and earth of Pisces-Virgo, to the air and fire of Aquarius-Leo.

The need to think in terms of pairs of opposites is not a peripheral matter and is the subject of much concern among astrologers today. As Sandra Levy says in *The Astrological Journal*: 'Recently there has been a lot said and written about the emergence of long-suppressed Virgo as the opposite sign and feminine principle of the Piscean Age. The extremism of Women's Lib and materialistic science are said to be two examples of this.'[19] She goes on to quote Liz Greene who says that as we move into the Aquarian age, it will only be by recognizing Leo, the feminine principle, that we will be able 'to heal the terrible split between the opposites which has occurred in the last age.'[20] Aquarius must not become split off from Leo in the new age in the way Pisces separated from Virgo in the last. On this analogy we may say that we must be open to Christ's new baptism 'with the Holy Spirit *and with fire.*'

An Aquarian exposition of the day of Pentecost

Having looked at these two possible forerunners of Aquarian spirituality, let us now go back to Acts 2 and examine the first eighteen verses in closer detail. Let us see whether they fit an Aquarian interpretation.

> Verses 1–2: When the day of Pentecost had fully come, they were all together in one place. And suddenly a sound came from heaven like the rush of a mighty wind, and it filled all the house where they were sitting.

The Hebrew word *ruach* and its Greek equivalent *pneuma* can be translated either as 'wind' or 'spirit.' The Spirit is of the air. It is in that sense Aquarian. The suddenness of its coming is like Uranus, the new ruler of Aquarius. As Alan Oken says: 'Uranus acts suddenly. It is unconventional, forceful, and often violent in its manner of expression.'[21]

> Verse 3: And there appeared to them tongues as of fire, distributed and resting on each one of them.

Here is the 'and with fire' we have just discussed. It is the sign of spiritual refining and the element of Leo.

> Verse 4: And they were filled with the Holy Spirit and began to speak in tongues, as the Spirit gave them utterance.

The actual phenomenon of speaking in other tongues is complex and controversial. Many studies for and against Pentecostal and Charismatic experiences have been written in recent years.[22] What is significant for us is that this 'unconventional' sign had a miraculous outcome — it enabled them all to understand each other's languages, as the story goes on to tell:

> Verses 5–8: Now there were dwelling in Jerusalem Jews, devout men from every nation under heaven. And at this sound the multitude came together, and they were bewildered, because each one heard them speaking in his own language. And they were amazed and wondered, saying, 'Are not all these who are speaking Galileans? And how is it that we hear, each of us in his own native language?'

This experience of all understanding in their own languages is usually thought of as an empowerment of the disciples for mission[23] and as the symbolic reversal of the experience at Babel where 'the Lord confused the language of all the earth' (Gen.11:9).[24] But it could also fit an Aquarian interpretation, for the Aquarian glyph: is the sign of communication. Unity, co-operation and synthesis are also some of its attributes, as Vera Reid explains: 'Its characteristics are unity, vision, memory, co-operation, synthesis ... and through it the three aspects of mind — consciousness, unconsciousness and super-consciousness seek simultaneous expression.'[25]

> Verses 9–11: Parthians and Medes and Elamites and residents of Mesopotamia, Judea and Cappadocia, Pontus and Asia, Phrygia and

Pamphylia, Egypt and the parts of Libya belonging to Cyrene, and
visitors from Rome, both Jews and proselytes, Cretans and Arabians,
we hear them telling in our own tongues the mighty works of God.

Scholars have often wondered why Luke chose such an odd list of
countries to represent 'every nation under heaven.' Attempts have been
made to find some symbolic order, most impressive of which, as J.W.
Packer points out 'is that based on astrological geography, whereby
each country is allotted to one of the signs of the zodiac.'[26] He goes
on to refer to the list drawn up by Paul of Alexandria in AD 378. This
list, given in full by Ernst Haenchen, is '1. Aries = Persia. 2. Taurus =
Babylon. 3. Gemini = Cappadocia. 4. Cancer = Armenia. 5. Leo = Asia
[Minor]. 6. Virgo = Hellas and Ionia. 7. Libra = Libya and Cyrene.
8. Scorpio = Italy. 9. Sagittarius = Cilicia and Crete. 10. Capricorn
= Syria. 11. Aquarius = Egypt. 12. Pisces = Red Sea and Indian
lands.'[27] Haenchen discusses this list at length, agreeing with Harnack,
Wellhausen and others that 'Judea' is a late addition.[28] Leaving that
out, it will be seen that Luke is in substantial agreement with Paul of
Alexandria. Gilles Quispel makes this clear by setting out the comparative lists:[29]

Zodiac	Paul of Alexandria	Acts
1. Aries	Persia	Parthians, Medes, Elamites
2. Taurus	Babylon	Mesopotamia
3. Gemini	Cappadocia	Cappadocia
4. Cancer	Armenia	Pontus
5. Leo	Asia Minor	Asia Minor
6. Virgo	Hellas and Ionia	Phrygia and Pamphylia
7. Libra	Libya and Cyrene	Libya and Cyrene
8. Scorpio	Italy	Rome
9. Sagittarius	Cilicia and Crete	Cretans
10. Capricorn	Syria	Judea
11. Aquarius	Egypt	Egypt
12. Pisces	Red Sea and India	Arabs

The list of countries then, like the twelve jewels in the foundation of New Jerusalem, indicates once again that there is far more astrological symbolism in the New Testament than is generally realized. This being so, it seems ever more reasonable to suppose that an Aquarian interpretation of Acts 2:1–18 is worthy of consideration, particularly as the universalism displayed there seems to be an Aquarian characteristic. Once again, Reid's description is remarkably apt: 'The true Aquarian knows no exclusive ties of race, colour, creed or family. To him all men are brothers and to all alike he extends the hand of friendship and goodwill.'[30]

> Verses 12–13: And all were amazed and perplexed, saying to one another, 'What does this mean?' But others mocking said, 'they are filled with new wine.'

The amazement, perplexity and shock that was experienced as some said 'What does this mean?' and others 'They are filled with new wine' continues to correspond to the comments which Oken makes about Uranus where he says this revolutionary and surprising planet 'tends to overthrow preconceived or conventional notions with its directness, originality, and intuitive perspective.'[31]

> Verses 14–17a: But Peter, standing with the eleven, lifted up his voice and addressed them, 'Men of Judea and all who dwell in Jerusalem, let this be known to you, and give ear to my words. For these men are not drunk, as you suppose, since it is only the third hour of the day; but this is what was spoken by the prophet Joel: 'And in the last days it shall be ...'

Peter gets up, asks for a hearing and starts to explain. He says that they are not drunk because it is too early in the day. No, this is the fulfilment of Joel's prophecy concerning the last days. Actually, Joel did not say 'in the last days,' but only 'afterward' or 'after these things.' Luke has changed the *meta tauta* of the Septuagint into *en tais eschatais hêmêrais*. Why has he done this? Robert Maddox suggests that he wanted to convey 'either that the consummation is imminent, for there are not many days to run before it comes, or else that the expected new age, the age when fulfilment of God's promises is actually experienced, has already arrived.'[32] All of which begins to look like another instance where 'in the last days' could be interpreted as 'at the end of the age' in the terms which we have already examined.

> Verse 17: 'And in the last days it shall be, God declares, that I will pour out my Spirit upon all flesh, and your sons and your daughters shall prophesy, and your young men shall see visions, and your old men shall dream dreams;

The Spirit is to be poured out 'upon all flesh.' It is universal.

In terms reminiscent of Teilhard de Chardin, Oken describes the 'water' which Aquarius pours out as 'the stream of universal consciousness, inspiration and intuition.' He goes on to say 'Aquarius, therefore, distributes the riches of life through an understanding of the nature of humanity.'[33] In other words he is very democratic. He distributes the riches of his inspiration among the sons and the daughters, the young and the old.

> Verse 18: Yea, and on my menservants and my maidservants in those days I will pour out my Spirit; and they shall prophesy.

He even distributes the gifts of his out-poured Spirit onto the servants, both men and women. Surely not on the slaves — and especially not on the *women* saves — how outrageous! How much more democratic — even Women's Lib — can you get? Well this is not surprising to the Aquarian, as Oken explains: 'Uranus is called the bohemian of the solar system because its vibrations demand freedom of behaviour on the personal level and the liberation of thought and movement from authoritarian control.'[34]

It seems strange, almost incongruous, that this Aquarian interpretation fits the story of Pentecost and Pentecostalism so well. This apparent incongruity stems from the fact that the Pentecostal and New Age movements view each other with deep suspicion. It is not too much to say that Pentecostals and Charismatics are liable to condemn New Agers as being of the devil, while the latter often think the former are narrow and bigoted. This is most unfortunate because, as has been shown, they have much in common and may be seen as authentic movements of the Spirit. This at least is the view of Kenneth Cuming, who suggests that if there is any devil's work afoot, it is in the division between them:

At the moment, another great upsurge of the Spirit is on its way. Within the Church itself, the great Charismatic movement of the Ministry of Healing is gathering momentum on all sides as many rush to join its ranks; the Pentecostal movement is likewise permeating all branches of the Church, whether Roman Catholic, Anglican or United Reform, and is sweeping through the Americas ... Outside the Church, the concept of another New Age dawning is being readily accepted, and New Age teachings promoted widely. Both are the promptings of the Holy Spirit, which is no respecter of persons. The two lines of approach should not be regarded as mutually incompatible, but rather as complementary and not antagonistic. For the Charismatic and Pentecostal movements are the spiritual-emotional wing; and the new schools of philosophy, science and psychology represent the spiritual-intellectual wing. Both together are thus the Wings of the Holy Spirit, and both have their allotted function in the New Age movement. Only the Devil wants them to be a 'house divided against itself.'[35]

If we were to continue this exposition of Acts 2, we would find that this chapter is just as Aquarian at its end as at its beginning, for in verses 44 and 45 it says: 'And all who believed were together and had all things in common; and they sold their possessions and goods and distributed them to all, as any had need.' This description of communal living corresponds exactly to the Aquarian characteristics of unity, co-operation and synthesis, already mentioned. As Vera Reid says, to the Aquarian: 'all men are brothers and to all alike he extends the hand of friendship.'

It could also be demonstrated that just as the Pentecostal experiences of Acts 2 are being reproduced on a massive scale in our time, so the Early Church's expression of unity and co-operation can also be found in many of the most significant movements of the last century. In the Church, for example, we could point to the ecumenical movement with its World Council of Churches, to the huge proliferation of basic Christian communities and to the growing House-Church movement. In international affairs we could instance the United Nations, the European Union and the Organization of African Unity. At the political and social levels various labour, socialist and co-operative movements stand out as obvious examples. Even Communism can be seen from this perspective as having been an extreme distorted expression of the same drive.

All these major movements, and many more, exemplify Aquarian attributes. They can also be seen as the varied successors of those who, having experienced the miracle of understanding each other 'in his own native language,' were led to have 'all things in common.' They can, in fact, be described as expressions of the Aquarian Spirit. As nations throughout the world strive towards democracy and unity; as churches experience community and overcome age-old divisions; as individual souls reject superannuated symbols and are baptized with fire and with the Holy Spirit, so we perceive the signs of a world Pentecost, an outpouring of the Spirit 'upon all flesh,' a planetary move towards the Age of Aquarius.

9. Christ: the Aquarian Logos

We have spent the last chapter identifying Aquarian symbolism and attributes in the New Testament and in the modern word. Our findings have centred on the second chapter of Acts, which would appear to be one which has central importance for our time. This is very significant, because it takes us back to the cycles of seven in the Jewish festivals, discussed in Chapter 4. After all, Pentecost — *pentekost*ê in Greek — means 'fiftieth' and was the name given to what in earlier times was called the Feast of Weeks. This, as we noted then, was one of the two biblical festivals, which had to be computed by counting seven times seven plus one. It seems extraordinary that, without any preconceived notion as to where our researches might lead, the hunt for Aquarius has landed us fairly and squarely back at one of the two festivals associated with the number fifty and at the only one literally called 'Fiftieth.'

This is even more remarkable when we realize that we could interpret Jubilee, the other festival associated with the number fifty, in exactly the same way. For the cause of Freedom — from Rousseau[1] to Martin Luther King,[2] from Wilberforce[3] to Liberation Theology[4] — has been just as important during the last two centuries as egalitarianism, and undoubtedly bears as close a resemblance to the Jubilee injunctions to 'proclaim liberty' and free the slaves (Lev.25), as socialism does to the Pentecostal imperative to have 'all things in common.' This Jubilee emphasis on freedom also fits an Aquarian interpretation, for its ruling planet Uranus 'demands freedom of behaviour on the personal level and liberation of thought and from authoritarian control.'[5] It would seem as though Uranus is just as much for freedom as equality and unity. In fact, according to Alan Oken, it turns out to be the complete revolutionary:

> The influence of Uranus through its revolutionary rays was felt in the United States in 1776, in France in 1789 ... When there was no great revolution of the masses, there was the Aquarian desire for unity and brotherhood ('Liberté, Fraternité, Egalité') ... Uranus' urge for freedom is always seen coupled with the desire for unification to take place within a given structure (Saturn).[6]

The Comma as metaphor for the age change

Why should it be that the principles associated with Pentecost and Jubilee should bear such striking similarities to those which have dominated our religious and political world more and more during the last two hundred years? Why is it that the truths associated with these two festivals appear to have the life-force of history in them for our time? Why is it that it is these two festivals, and no others, which are so closely connected with the number fifty? Is the number fifty, in this sense, important for the understanding of our time?

I believe the answer to all these questions can be found in an understanding of our times as the 'age change,' the tumultuous period on the cusp between the Ages of Pisces and Aquarius. As we discovered in Chapter 4, in music the number fifty is associated both with harmony and with harmonic imperfection. The discrepancy between seven octaves and twelve fifths, the Pythagorean Comma, by analogy therefore speaks of both humankind's quest for the perfection of harmony and at the same time of the discord by which he finds himself surrounded. It is this paradoxical musical analogy which aptly describes this period of the 'age change' from Pisces to Aquarius, because the former is associated with the discord of dualism and the latter with the concord of a holistic view of things. As Carl Jung says:

> If, as seems probable, the aeon of the fishes is ruled by the archetypal motif of the hostile brothers, then the approach of the next Platonic month, namely Aquarius, will constellate the problem of the union of opposites.[7]

Paradoxically, therefore, the Comma represents 'the problem of the union of opposites' — the problem of overcoming dualism with harmony, of reconciling the hostile brothers. Liz Greene, in *Relating*, speaks of the dualism of the Piscean Age as being not only inherent in the sign of the two fishes swimming in opposite directions but also in the hostility between Pisces and its polar opposite Virgo. We have touched on this in Chapter 8 but most now go into it in greater detail:

> But the values embodied by Pisces and its opposite sign, Virgo, have been inimical to each other for the last two thousand years. This enmity is very similar to that experienced by an individual at

war with his own shadow. The qualities embodied by Virgo were
forcibly repressed during the Piscean age. In consequence, the
highest value — that absolute love for and forgiveness of mankind
of which Christ is the most significant symbol — has not been given
balance and form by the realistic earthy consciousness of Virgo.[8]

She goes on to identify 'the enormous implications in this terrible split
in the collective unconscious of man in the Piscean era.' It has been a time
when Virgo, the symbol of Woman, has been 'charged with the projec-
tion of the collective shadow,' with darkness, the demonic, weakness and
inferiority. The Holy Trinity has been seen as masculine 'while woman,
matter, earth, remains below, in the grip of the Lord of the World.'[9]

In contrast she says that we are now approaching the new age in
which this 'terrible split' will be overcome. There will be the possibility
of a union of opposites, but only if the Aquarian consciousness does not
repress or reject its polar opposite Leo, the way Pisces treated Virgo:

We may see words leaking into common speech which show
us how far the new values have progressed: in the Piscean age,
one spoke of love, compassion, selflessness and sacrifice, while
now we speak of group consciousness, energy, organization
and discovery. Aquarius, with all its nobility, will wipe out the
individual if it runs rampant; Leo, if it is suppressed and erupts,
is the dictator, the megalomaniac, the true figure of the antichrist,
whose individuality is the supreme value. Somewhere between
these two we must steer our course.[10]

It is now possible to see from what Liz Greene says, that, just as
the experience and ethics of Pentecost and Jubilee offer us a model
with which to interpret the history of the last two hundred years, so the
spiritual truths symbolized by the Pythagorean Comma offer us a psy-
chological way of analyzing the age change from Pisces to Aquarius.
The number fifty, with all its musical and spiritual ambiguities, could
therefore very well be the number that epitomizes this time of transition from the dissonances of Piscean dualism to the consonances of the
Aquarian union of opposites.

The time and effort we have expended in attempting to understand
the Comma, may now be proving to have been well worthwhile if
it is giving us such a complex and profound metaphor for the basic

consciousness of our age. David Tame, speaking of the comma, told us earlier that 'The cycle of twelve perfect fifths did not *close* and finish a cycle of seven octaves, but exceeded it, and thus, as it were, spiralled *upward*,'[11] and Herbert Whone similarly said 'the fifth overshooting the mark opens the door to an infinity of frequencies.'[12] This upward spiral, 'this infinity of frequencies' is our analogy for the period of the cusp of the ages in which we now find ourselves. It is this very discrepancy, which appears to be our hope, our freedom and our future. For it is only a Comma, not a full stop — an age change, not an apocalypse. It is the very instability that propels us forward, the off-balancing impulse that moves all things onwards. It is the upward spiral of the galaxies, of DNA, of phyllotaxis, of all growth and movement. It seems as though it could indeed be identified with the very pulse of life, which we explored in Chapter 5. If this is the case then it would certainly explain the centrality of the Spirit in both Pentecost and Jubilee. It would also confirm Tame's staggering assertion, quoted in Chapter 5, that 'it is by the phenomenon of Pythagoras' Comma that the very nature of our lives within the realm of mortality is arranged.'[13]

The Logos and Aquarian spirituality

I believe we can find a close link between what we have just been saying about the harmonious union of opposites and an important New Testament understanding of who Jesus was, which so far we have only touched on and must now examine more fully. This is further emphasized by Liz Greene where she says:

> We now talk about archetypes and energy rather than gods; to Aquarius, everything is energy and operates according to natural laws, and these energies exist within as well as outside man. God, to Aquarius, is the intelligent principle by which these laws, both physical and psychic operate.[14]

If we amalgamate Greene's description of the Aquarian perception of God as 'the intelligent principle' of natural laws, with Jung's 'union of opposites,' we get something remarkably similar to the ancient concept of the Logos, the Word, as defined by its originator, the Greek philosopher Heraclitus (535–475 BC). George S. Hendry, in *Theology of Nature* explains:

Heraclitus was interested in the process of change itself, and he sought to discover the law or principle that governs it. He found it in the conflict of opposites which, despite their opposition, interact harmoniously, according to the regulation of a principle, which he called the Logos and invested with divine attributes.[15]

This original definition of the Logos is clearly very like Greene's and Jung's Aquarian understanding of God. This likeness becomes even more marked when we realize that Heraclitus invented the word 'harmony' (*harmonia*), to explain what he meant by the balance of conflicting opposites brought about by the Logos.[16] The similarity between the two systems of thought is remarkable and appears to agree to a great extent with much that we have been discovering in the course of this enquiry, not only about the number fifty and the Pythagorean Comma, but also about the music of the spheres, the harmonic universe, the measures of Solomon's temple and the consonances of the cube of the New Jerusalem. It seems, therefore, that we may rightfully ascribe all these Aquarian and harmonious attributes to Jesus Christ himself because, according to the famous prologue to John's gospel, he was the incarnation of the Logos:[17]

> In the beginning was the word [*Logos*], and the Word [*Logos*] was with God, and the Word [*Logos*] was God. He was in the beginning with God; all things were made through him, and without him was not anything made that was made.

It is surprising how quickly we have moved from what perhaps might have appeared to be no more than astrological and musicological speculations, to the interpretation of this key New Testament text. For key text this was, at least in the Early Church, as the writings of the Fathers such as Justin Martyr, Irenaeus, Tertullian, Clement of Alexandria, Origen, Eusebius and many others show. Justin Martyr called Heraclitus 'a Christian before Christ' on the strength of it.[18] Irenaeus saw Christ as the proportion or 'measure of the Father'[19] and Eusebius went even further in his Christianizing of *harmonia* in his *Demonstratio Evangelica*. The Logos, he said:

> ... always continuously pervades the whole matter of the elements and of actual bodies; and, as being creator — word of God,

stamps on it the principles (*logoi*) of the wisdom derived from Him. He impresses life on what is lifeless and form on what is in itself formless and indeterminate, reproducing in the qualities of the bodies, the values and the unembodied forms inherent in Him; He sets into all-wise and all harmonious motion things that are on their own account lifeless and immobile — earth, water, fire, and air: He orders everything out of disorder, giving development and completion: with the actual power of deity and logos He all but forces all things: He pervades all things and grasps all things, yet contracts no injury from nor is sullied in himself.[20]

In the context of this study, this passage must be regarded as an extraordinarily accurate and comprehensive description of the cosmic Christ. Eusebius has stolen my lines! This is Christ the Creator, the Pantocrator, as Paul called him.[21] This is the Christ of cosmology. It also reads like a commentary on Colossians (1:15–17), where Paul speaks of Christ as 'the first-born of all creation:'

He is the image of the invisible God, the first-born of all creation; for in him all things were created, in heaven and on earth, visible and invisible, whether thrones or dominions or principalities or authorities — all things were created through him and for him. He is before all things, and in him all things hold together.

Paul's description is very like Eusebius' 'He pervades all things and grasps all things.' It is also very like Greene's where she says: 'God, to Aquarius is the intelligent principle by which these laws, both physical and psychic operate.'

If the Early Church Fathers gave such centrality to this definition of Christ, then why did it not continue to occupy a position of central importance? There were many reasons for this but broadly speaking scholars agree that the Logos concept proved to be too vague and imprecise to express the subtle distinctions of the complex christological debates of the third and fourth centuries. It could mean too many things, it was tainted with too many gnostic associations and its universalism became increasingly suspect. G.L. Prestige says: 'the doctrine of the Logos, great as was its importance for theology, harboured deadly perils in its bosom,'[22] and T.E. Pollard asserts 'In the Arian and Marcellan controversies, the inadequacy of the Logos-concept, however it is to be interpreted, as the basis for Christian thinking about Jesus Christ, is revealed.'[23] Maurice Wiles adds that compared with the graphic and personal notion of Christ as 'the Son of the Father,' the Logos was pale and abstract: 'Logos was a scholar's term; it was not well fitted to meet the religious needs of ordinary folk.'[24] To these reasons we may add that the holistic and inclusive concept of the Logos proved increasingly inimical to the rise of Piscean ecclesiastical dualism.

For all these reasons, from the second half of the third century onwards, the mind of the Church moved slowly but firmly away from the belief that the Logos could be in creation or in humankind, even to a small degree, in the same way as it was in Christ. Maurice Wiles speaks of this fateful development:

> The attempt to frame a theology of the divine Christ in terms of the Logos of God was a failure, but it was a noble failure. It was never fiercely repudiated, not totally abandoned; but it did gradually lose the centre of the stage. Theology underwent a gradual change of emphasis rather than a sudden reversal of direction. Many of the ideas, which it had suggested, lived on in new settings. Some of these, which were eventually lost, were lost to the detriment of the Church's thought and life. The idea of a link between the universal Logos incarnate in Christ and the fragmentary Logos present in every man, provides a dimension to Christian theology which has often been unhappily absent.[25]

As Wiles says: 'the idea of a link between the universal Logos incarnate in Christ and the fragmentary Logos present in every man ... has often been unhappily absent.' However, if we have been justified in seeing a close connection between this ancient concept and the new spiritual consciousness of Aquarius, this should change. We should expect to see a return to the belief that the Logos, which was incarnate in Christ, is also to some degree present in all humanity and in all creation. We should also expect to find a resurgence of belief in the incarnate Logos himself, the cosmic Christ. And this is indeed what is beginning to happen all over the world in this generation. There is an awakening to a new awareness of the universality of Christ's presence and power. Horizons are being widened and vision is being extended. On the cusp of the ages, the Aquarian Logos is revealing the truths of the ancient wisdom. He is giving:

... true understanding of things as they are: a knowledge of the structure of the world and the operation of the elements; the beginning and the end of epochs and their middle course; the alternating solstices and changing seasons; the cycles of the years and the constellations. (Wis.Sol.7:17–19 NEB)

Through this revelation of the knowledge of the structure and cycles of the cosmos 'as they are,' he is leading us to a new awareness of the point our planet has reached in cosmic time. We are beginning to be able to read the ominous signs of our times not as the countdown to catastrophe but as the birth pangs of a new epoch of creation. For, as Liz Greene reminds us, 'Astrological ages appear to commence with great heaves and groans, like the birth of any new thing into the world, and they are accompanied by the death pangs of the old era which engendered them.'[26]

This is the message of hope for a confused and frightened world. There is a long-term future for us to which we can and should commit ourselves. It involves the acceptance of change, the willingness to work for, not against, nature, and the ability to see things whole. In this transition period we must seek to align ourselves 'with the set of the celestial tides'[27] so that the conflict of opposites may be overcome and the true harmony of Christ be established in all things.

10. New Age Piscean Jesus

The previous chapters of this book were first published under the title *Christ and the Cosmos* in February 1986. A year later, my wife and I found ourselves re-employed by the Church of Scotland, this time by the Overseas Department. We were appointed to run their Sea of Galilee Centre in Tiberias, Israel. Seeing many of the sites associated with the Galilean ministry of Jesus afresh, through the interpretative lens of *Christ and the Cosmos*, particularly the chapters 'Great New Year's Day' and 'Ichthus: the Great Fish' was very exciting. I had gone to Israel wondering, among other things, whether my theory that Jesus had been a New Age Piscean would stand the test of my experience on site. I was conscious that I had not as yet been able to answer this question satisfactorily back home in my study. Did Jesus, in his person and teachings, in his words and actions, in his ethic and consciousness, embody the spirit and attributes of the then New Age of Pisces? Could he be easily recognized as a New Age Piscean as distinct from an Old Age Arian? If so, how could this be discerned? Before describing how I experienced very positive answers to these questions I would like to reiterate an astrological point made previously by Liz Greene.

The Ages of Aries-Libra and Pisces-Virgo

The point was made earlier in the book that astrologers hold that because there are only six axes in the zodiac, each sign must be regarded with its opposite or complementary sign (see Chapter 8). Thus instead of saying that the star of Bethlehem ended the Age of Aries, we should more precisely have said the Age of Aries-Libra and instead of saying that it ushered in the Age of Pisces, we should more properly have said the Age of Pisces-Virgo.

Liz Greene maintained that there had not only been a tragic dualism inherent in the Piscean Age with the two fishes swimming in opposite directions, but also that there had been a deep hostility between Pisces and its complementary sign Virgo. She said that the challenge of the new Age of Aquarius was to achieve a balance of opposites with its complementary sign Leo.

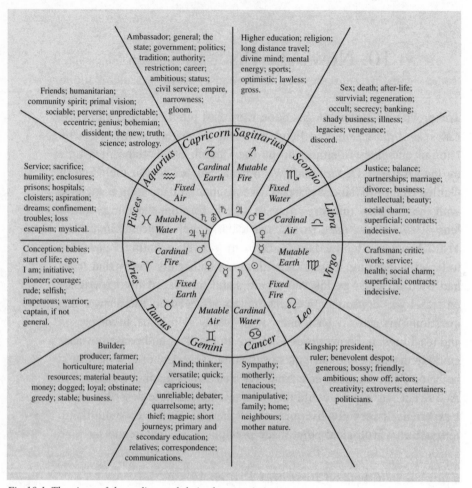

Fig.10.1. The signs of the zodiac and their characteristics.

You will see from the illustration above that the sign of Aries, the Ram, in the first house is said to 'rule' conception, babies, the start of life, the ego and the 'I am' consciousness. Its characteristics are, positively: initiative, pioneering spirit, courage and the officer-like qualities of the military captain if not the general. Negatively its qualities are said to be rudeness, selfishness and reckless impetuosity.

If you look across the zodiac to Libra, the Scales, the complementary sign of Aries, you will find that it is a Cardinal Air sign ruled by Venus. Its main rulership is of justice, partnerships, marriage, divorce and business contracts. You will also see that Libra's main positive attributes are intellect, beauty and social charm but whose negative ones are said to include superficiality, indecision and a legalistic interpretation of justice.

Let us now look at Pisces, the Fish, or rather fishes, the changeable water sign which rules the twelfth, last house, whose old ruler is Jupiter and whose new ruler is Neptune. Here, we have a very different scenario. As Vera Reid said in Chapter 6, Aries rules the head but Pisces rules the feet, so in the analogy of the parts of the body, we move from the seat of pride to the seat of humility for the head, though clever, is proud, while the feet are always humble servants. So Pisces rules service, sacrifice and humility, and is associated with the traditional institutions where these qualities may find their best expression: hospitals, religious cloisters, schools and prisons. Through Neptune's influence it is also considered to be the most spiritual sign, being dreamy and mystical. However, it has a downside which includes escapism, alcoholism, drugs and troubles in general. This is so much the case that it is sometimes described by one difficult word: loss.

Looking across the zodiac to Pisces' opposite or complementary sign, Virgo, the Virgin, we find a mutable, Earth sign ruled traditionally by Mercury but more recently — according to an increasing number of astrologers — by Chiron, the new planet discovered or re-discovered in 1977. Chiron is known as the Wounded Healer, and the fact that it has been ascribed to Virgo shows how much the latter should truly complement Pisces. For Virgo, among other things, also rules service, particularly with regard to health and healing. Thus doctors, nurses and all those doing practical, caring work, are said to be ruled by Virgo. The downside of this sign is said to be characterized by the over-critical teacher, the nit-picking bureaucrat and the fuss-pot for domestic tidiness.

With this simple, perhaps *simplistic*, introduction to the qualities and attributes of the Aries-Libra and the Pisces-Virgo axes, we are now in a position to understand the story of how I came to the conviction that Jesus, in his life and work, his sayings and actions, did indeed fit the model of the Pisces-Virgo, not the Aries-Libra, Messiah and how he may therefore be said to have embodied the eschatological expectations and fulfilled the prophetic hopes of the long looked-forward to, blessed Age which was about to begin.

Fig.10.2. Mosaic at the Church of Multiplication at Tabgha, Sea of Galilee.

Pisces-Virgo symbolism by the Sea of Galilee

On a tour round the pilgrim sites at the North end of the Sea of Galilee
I began to see everything in the light of Jesus as the New Age Piscean;
more precisely as the Piscean-Virgoan Messiah of the New Cosmic
Axis; of the New Great Year.

In the Church of the Multiplication at Tabgha was the top of the
original rock on which Jesus was reputed to have laid, blessed and
multiplied the loaves and fishes. There was also the famous mosaic of
a basket with the loaves in it, flanked by the two fish, which I remembered from my previous visits. As soon as I saw this I said to myself
'Pisces-Virgo! The fish are for Pisces and the loaves are for Virgo who
is Ceres, the corn goddess.' It seemed obvious. Jesus was the Great
Fish ICHTHUS, *Iesous Christos*, *Theou*, *Huios*, *Soter*. The first letters
of: Jesus Christ, Son of God, Saviour, the creed of the early Church,
in Greek, spelt *Ichthus*, the Greek for fish (see Chapter 7). I perceived
Virgo, the complementary sign to Pisces, 'Born of the Virgin Mary,' as
the archetype of the earth's abundance, particularly grain. Pisces and
Virgo together were the signs of the New Age and of the Axis which
dawned at the birth of Jesus. The symbolism struck me forcibly.

The next stop on our tour was less than a mile away, the Mount of
Beatitudes, where somewhere on the gently sloping hillside below us

the fourth-century pilgrim Egeria, maintained that Jesus had preached the sermon on the mount. As the Beatitudes were read out it seemed to me that I heard the voice of one proclaiming that the attributes of the New Age of Pisces-Virgo had both superseded and fulfilled those of the old age of Aries-Libra: 'Blessed are those who are poor in spirit, ... who mourn, ... are meek, ... hunger and thirst for righteousness, ... are merciful, ... pure in heart, ... peacemakers, ... persecuted for right-eousness' sake.' These ethical qualities spoke of a new dispensation. There is nothing harsh, no 'thou shalt nots,' no tit for tats, about them. Quite the contrary. They are mild, yielding and irenic, and demonstrate the differences between Aries and Pisces, between cardinal fire and mutable water attributes, between the most assertive masculine and the most passive of the feminine signs of the zodiac. The contrasts between the old law and the new were repeatedly enumerated by Jesus in the many times he stated 'You have heard that it was said of old ... But I say to you ...' Each time he made this distinction, the 'you have heard ...' corresponded to an Aries or Libran principle and the 'But I say' to a Piscean or Virgoan one, for example: 'You have heard that it was said, "An eye for an eye and a tooth for a tooth" (Libra). But I say to you, Do not resist one who is evil (Pisces). But if anyone strikes you on the right cheek (Aries) turn to him the other also' (Pisces) (Matt.5:38f). 'You have heard that it was said "You shall love your neighbour and hate your enemy." (Aries) But I say to you, Love your enemies and pray for all those who persecute you ...' (Pisces)

Once I had seen this clearly, I read on in Matthew and realized afresh that the gospel narrative contains even more miracles of healing than teaching, sermons or parables. In Matthew 8 alone there is the cleansing of the leper, the healing of the centurion's servant and Peter's mother-in-law. This particular passage finishes with 'That evening they brought to him many who were possessed with demons; and he cast out the spirits with a word, and healed all who were sick.' (Matt.8:16) Was it more than coincidence that Virgo rules doctors, nurses, health and the physical body? And was it more than coincidence that Pisces rules hospitals and sacrificial love? Certainly the parable of the Good Samaritan epitomizes the best of Virgoan and Piscean qualities. I could also see how Jesus himself incarnated these qualities in a supreme way. His anointing, his messiahship, was not that he might display military strength and subdue all his enemies by conquest as King David had done and as the zealot nationalists wanted him to do. It was not an Aries messiahship to which he had been called. No, it was Piscean salvation which he embodied, which he learned about from the great prophets of the outer Piscean cusp of the sixth century BC, especially Isaiah, who proclaimed in his early controversial sermon in Nazareth: 'The Spirit of the Lord ... has anointed me to preach good news to the *poor*, to proclaim release to the *captives*, recovery of sight to the *blind* and liberty for the *oppressed*.' (Isa.61:1f) He was in fact proclaiming the Year of Jubilee (see Chapter 4).

My astrological speculations wouldn't leave me alone and preoccupied me until we returned to Tiberias. Reading more of the gospels in this light, it seemed ever clearer that the incomprehension of the disciples, who appear to have been so slow to understand what their master was really getting at, was because they couldn't change their expectation of what the messiah should have been like and what he should have done, from an Aries-Libran model to a Piscean-Virgoan one. They found it almost impossible to shift their messianic paradigm. Likewise the religious opposition either felt let down, like the Pharisees, because Jesus wouldn't play the nationalist card and lead a political revolt, or were frightened, like the Chief Priests, who were Herodians at heart, that that was precisely what he would do. The whole drama of the New Testament seemed to me to centre round a new set of values, embodied in Jesus, appearing suddenly in the middle of a highly conservative religious scene in which the old set of values did not wish to be upstaged or superseded. To the vast majority, although they loved his miraculous power and thought he was a superb preacher, the idea of their hero being an apparent wimp was not appealing. If only he would have used his amazing gifts to lead from the front and knock hell out of the Romans and the Herodians. But his power was only to be used to help and persuade, not to coerce or conquer.

There were so many sayings utterly central to the message and lifestyle of Jesus that seemed to fit this interpretation, it was almost overwhelming. Three in particular struck me: 'He who is greatest among you shall be your servant, whoever exalts himself will be humbled and whoever humbles himself shall be exalted' (Matt.23:11). Here the concept of power which, with Aries, had been associated with political rulership and strong-arm tactics, is turned upside down and equated with Piscean humility and servanthood. 'If any man would come after me let him deny himself and take up his cross daily and follow me. For whoever would save his life will lose it and whoever loses his life for my sake will save it.' (Luke 9:24) This paradox of winning through losing, of gain through loss, juxtaposes the competitive individualism of Aries with the collective social responsibility of Pisces. The strength of Aries now had to be made perfect through the apparent weakness of Pisces. 'Jesus rose from supper, laid aside his garments, and girded himself with a towel. Then he poured water into a basin, and began to wash the disciples' feet, and to wipe them with the towel with which he was girded.' (John 13:3–5) As already mentioned Aries rules the head and wears the crown, but Pisces rules the feet which need washing. There is no greater distance in the human body than from the head to the feet. What a comedown! Simon Peter resisted having his feet washed, just as he had resisted Jesus when he said he had to suffer many things and be rejected. If each of the disciples represented a zodiac sign, then Peter must have been Aries, the head, the impulsive, assertive, unreliable leader. He had to learn slowly and painfully about Piscean service, humility and sacrifice.

I felt that I had also discovered why the north-west corner of the Sea of Galilee had been chosen by Jesus to be the initial focus of his Galilean ministry. It was because it was the only place in the whole land where the produce of the sea (Pisces) and the fertility of the earth (Virgo) came together so closely and in such profusion. At Tabgha, the place of Seven Springs, were hot streams flowing into the Lake. This area was *the* fishing ground for the fishermen of Capernaum, because the fish are attracted to the warmer water where it enters the Lake and are thus easily caught. Likewise the plain of Gennersaret, stretching south from Tabgha for a few miles to Magdala, was then — and has become once again — one of the most fruitful areas in the whole of soil-rich Galilee. George Adam Smith's *The Historical Geography of the Holy Land*, states that since ancient times, this plain had been regarded as the quintessence of the luxuriant growth of nature in its variety of gardens, fruit and grain. Josephus, writing only a few years after Jesus, said of it:

> One may call this place the ambition of Nature, where it forces plants, natural enemies, to agree together: it is a happy contention of the seasons, as if each of them laid claim to this country, for it not only nourishes different sorts of autumnal fruits beyond men's expectation, but preserves them a great while. It supplies men with the principal fruits, grapes and figs, continually during ten

months, and the rest of the fruits, as they ripen together through the whole year. (*Wars*, 3.10.8)

It was in effect, a little Eden from the produce of which he who came to be called the second Adam, chose the loaves of bread through which he manifested his power to feed the multitude, and which he later used to speak of himself as the Bread of Life. The coming together of such rich abundance of fish and fruitfulness, the harvest of water and earth was the perfect place for the proclamation of the New Age of Pisces-Virgo.

I couldn't also help noticing that the ancient site of Kinnereth, which gave and still gives its name to the Lake itself, lay in that Edenic plain. The name is derived from *kinnor* the Hebrew equivalent of the Greek *kithara*, the harp or lyre. The symbolism here seemed just as obvious. Jesus, as the new King David had come to play not on the outward harp but on the inner strings of the soul and had come to restore the lost harmony to all things.

We worked for two years at Tiberias and having seen clearly the Piscean-Virgoan characteristics in the life and teaching of Jesus, I came to see just as clearly that I was surrounded by a conflict in which both sides believed so passionately in the qualities of the Age of Aries-Libra that they were inevitably finding themselves re-enacting the historical conflicts of the Old Testament. I came to think that this re-enactment of the political history of the early books of the Bible, as if nothing had changed during the intervening three thousand years, was one of the greatest tragedies of the modern world.

11. The Twelve Epochs of
the Age of Pisces

You will remember that after establishing the principles of spatial harmonics which lay behind the cubic structure of the New Jerusalem and the string-length ratios of Solomon's Temple, we went on to establish an equivalent harmonic structure with regard to *time*. It was explained in Chapter 4, 'Cycles of Seven and the Jewish Festivals,' that the annual cycle of the Hebrew Festivals followed a harmonic pattern in which each month was regarded as a semitone of an Octave Year and that the seven major festivals, falling harmonically in the first, third and seventh semitone-months thus 'played' the minor triad on the Octave-Year. This then led on from the yearly cycle to the Jubilee cycle of forty-nine and fifty years and from there to the largest time cycle of all, the Great Year of 25,920 years, its 'months' or Ages of 2,160 years and its 'days' of seventy-two years.

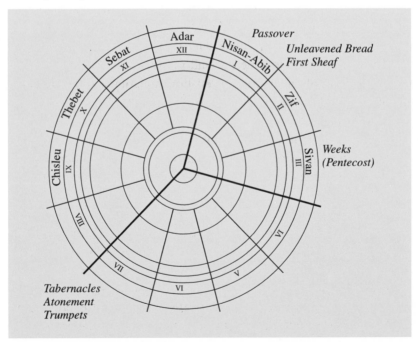

Fig.11.1. The festivals as the minor triad.

To be true to this intimate connection between space and time, we would have to find a harmonic pattern of time which could be recognized as the macrocosmic equivalent to the 'Octave' Year of twelve 'Semitone' months. This would appear to be a very difficult task because, while it is legitimate today for theoretical physicists to seek for a 'theory of everything' in spatial terms, to do so in temporal terms, would be regarded as madness. For while today we are all wedded to the belief that the universe can be analysed legitimately in terms of spatial patterns, such as the dodecahedron or icosahedron, we are equally wedded to the belief that it cannot be so analysed with regard to temporal patterns such as Ages, Epochs or Eras, at least not with the same degree of precision. This is one of the reasons why astrology, which aims to do exactly this, is viewed by most with such deep suspicion. Yet we have seen in our analysis of the Age of Pisces and Aquarius, and especially in the dating of the birth of Christ by the Saturn-Jupiter conjunction in 6 BC, that such a precision can at least be approached.

Can we go any further towards a greater precision? Many astrologers themselves are dubious about the use of the Ages of the Great Year for dating history because they say it is too vague, the time span being too long. They disagree widely on the exact date when one Age ends and another begins and so it must follow that all other dates will be imprecise. Charles Carter, a famous political astrologer of the mid-twentieth century, was one of these, saying with regard to the start of the New Age that 'it would indeed be difficult to assert with assurance when the First Point will enter the constellation Aquarius and the so-called and much heralded Aquarian Age will begin.' However, despite his reservations, he noted that cycles had played a large part in historical astrology and that the succession of 'periods' ruled by the planets had been prominent in Hindu predictive astrology. He also admitted that astrologically, there *are* periods or epochs and that it is important to study them:

> However, it is certain that periods or epochs do occur and can be correlated with the signs. This will, I believe, be quite clear to those who have the astrological knowledge that will indicate to them what should be looked for. These periods are not only intensely interesting historically, but they also provide a background for all social and political studies, dominating as they do the entire life of their times.

What is of enormous relevance to our enquiries, is that after accepting the existence of historical-astrological periods and their importance, he then solves the difficulty regarding the precise start-point of the Age of Pisces by quite simply claiming that *for him* it started at the year of the birth of Christ:

> We begin, then, from AD 1 or thereabouts. The exact date of Jesus' birth is uncertain, but a matter of a few years is of small importance, for *Natura non agit per saltum* and we shall always find that one epoch tends to pass somewhat gradually into the next.

He then goes on to divide the Age of Pisces into twelve epochs of 180 years, beginning with the birth of Christ and limiting himself to an outline of European history.

In so doing he has provided us with a macrocosmic equivalent to the Twelve Semitone months of the Octave Year. If we place the semitones of the scale of C round the start dates which he gives for the twelve epochs, we can begin to speculate how different notes or chords could be associated with different epochs in the development of western music. The notes of other scales such as D or E might fit better and it would take a trained musicologist, or an experienced harmonic astrologer, to work out exactly what musical vibrations correspond to astrological epochs and the relationships between them. This must be left to another occasion. However, it is sufficient here merely to establish the principle of harmonic periods of time and to at least acknowledge the department of astrological studies known as harmonic astrology.

As an example of the associations with musical-historical epochs that would begin to authenticate this theory, we could note that the minor seventh rests on the year 1800, introducing the Epoch of Aquarius. This saw the beginning of the High Romantic period, which at least in part is associated with unrequited, romantic love. The unresolved nature of the minor seventh fits this emotional condition extremely well and appropriately can be found in Beethoven, and other Romantic composers from around 1800, culminating in Wagner's 'Tristan Chord' of infinite longing, which uses the minor seventh to supreme effect.

Just how convincing Charles Carter's theory of Epochs is, can only be demonstrated by his essay on the subject which first appeared in

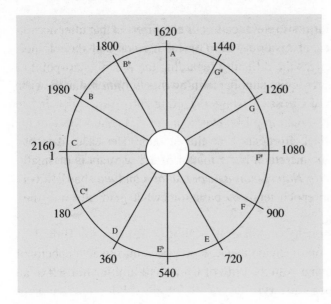

Fig.11.2. Carter's twelve Piscean epochs and the twelve semitone months of the Octave Year.

Astrology magazine for December 1947 under the title 'Historical Cycles and Newly Found Planets.'[1] We will now look at a summary of this, to which I have added some of my own observations.

Carter's historical evidence for twelve Piscean epochs

In dividing the Age of Pisces into the twelve epochs of 180 years Carter says modestly that by so doing 'we may find ourselves able to carry out some useful researches into the correspondences that may be found between these epochs and the accepted values of the twelve zodiacal signs (or constellations).'

1. The first epoch, AD 1–180, is that of the first sign Aries, the Ram, which is a cardinal fire sign ruled by Mars. It is the sign of the warrior, initiator and pioneer. Carter saw these qualities manifest supremely in the aggressive expansion of the Roman Empire under the despotism of the Caesars:

> This first epoch covers the period of the Caesars and their successors Nerva, Trajan, Hadrian and the two Antonines. It was a period during which absolute power lay in the hands of one man and that power was hardly disputed. ... It was an age of complete

despotism except in so far as it was tempered by the fear of assassination or military revolt. This agrees well with Aries.

What Carter says about the Caesars is strangely mirrored in the birth and growth of the Christian Church. During the Aries epoch it had great energy and spread to all known countries. The Apostles and the Seventy-Two had the missionary drive of Aries pioneers. The Apostolic and post-Apostolic periods saw the soldiers of Christ fight many a spiritual battle while the cult of martyrdom, led by such figures as Polycarp and Justin, made heroes out of the fallen.

2. The second epoch, AD 180–360, is that of Taurus, the Bull. This is a fixed earth sign ruled by Venus and is associated with the builder, the farmer, material resources and physical beauty. Carter observes that it begins in 180 with the death of the philosopher-emperor Marcus Aurelius, and that it was from this event that Gibbon dated the beginning of *The Decline and Fall of the Roman Empire*. The series of defeats at the hands of the barbarians (apart from the reign of Diocletian) signalled the end of the dominant influence of Aries, while the development of garrison legions building defences and 'digging in,' supported by an expanding bureaucracy, marked the increase of imperial stability in a very Taurean way. However, this eventually led to stagnation and decline.

On the religious side of things Carter notes the rise of the cult of Mithras, the Bull-slayer throughout the Roman Empire, and also the strong influence of a Platonic and Pythagorean philosophical revival. These movements ran contemporaneously with the spread of Christianity and, taken all together, showed that 'an ideal of saintliness had come into men's minds that would have seemed strange and unintelligible to the pagans of a century before.'

On the political scene at this time, Carter notes the important revival of the Persian Empire. This he believes is because Persia is ruled by Taurus:

Now Persia is under Taurus, and it is very natural that in any given epoch, countries that come under the same sign-value as the epoch will in some respect experience an augmentation.

3. The third epoch, 360–540, is that of Gemini, the Twins. It is a mutable air sign ruled by Mercury. Being an air sign and mutable Gemini displays the mercurial qualities of quick-wittedness, a magpie energy for collecting disparate knowledge and a passion for debate and/ or argument. It rules primary and secondary education, communications and short journeys. Carter associates it with duality for the twins argue continuously and are often divided. This is exemplified by the Emperor Valentinian who, in 364, took the fateful step of dividing the Empire, giving the eastern part to his brother. The final division came after Justinian the Great (527–65).

Under the epoch of Gemini he also puts the rise of the Germanic races. This is of great importance to him and indeed to us:

> Perhaps the most striking thing about this period, from the general European point of view, was the dominance of the Germanic races. During the Taurus age they had perpetually harassed the Empire; now they flooded over it and left their traces in France, Spain, Northern Italy and even Africa. Tacitus says of the Germans that they worshipped Mercury before all other gods, and so this development seems in agreement with our hypothesis.

In Church history striking expressions of the Geminian capacity for argument can be seen in the seemingly endless debates about exactly who Jesus was, how he should be described in credal formulae and who should be regarded as heretical! These debates were often fierce and acrimonious leaving lasting wounds and divisions in the Body of Christ. This was certainly the case with regard to Athanasius and the Athanasian Creed of 362; the Council of Ephesus regarding the doctrine of the motherhood of God in 431, the final adoption of the Nicene Creed and the definitive Christological formulae decided upon at the Council of Chalcedan in 451.

4. The fourth epoch is that of Cancer, the Crab, 540–720. This is a cardinal water sign ruled by the moon. It is the sign of the mother and maternal qualities. It rules the family and the home as well as Mother Nature and mother church. Carter sees the rise of the papacy under Pope Gregory the Great from 590 as very Cancerian, as well as the great influence which Justinian's wife exerted on the Emperor Justinian:

One might expect some great female figures to occur during these times, but this was, of course, something that could not easily occur, taking into account the general level of civilisation. However, one of the most famous monarchs of the time, Justinian, was notoriously wife-ruled. The same emperor has come down to us made famous by the legal codification that took place under his auspices and perhaps that has some connection with the exaltation of Jupiter in Cancer. It is the office of the law to protect the innocent and this protective aspect is quite Cancerian.

Carter also notes the rise of what he calls *Muhammadenism*, but without comment. In this he reveals himself to be very much a man of his times, but may perhaps be forgiven for such a cursory mention because strictly speaking Islam would fall outside the scope of European history. However, this would not be tolerated today when Islam is increasingly recognized as having been an integral part of European development. For the purposes of this brief outline it is sufficient to mention that under the flag of the Cancerian crescent moon, Muslim armies had conquered Arabia, Egypt, Syria, Palestine, Iraq, Iran, Afghanistan, North Africa and Spain by the end of this Epoch. They had become a force to be reckoned with throughout the world, including Europe.

5. The fifth epoch is that of Leo, the Lion, 720–900. This is a fixed fire sign ruled by the sun, and is associated with kingship and fatherhood. It rules creativity, entertaining, acting and politicians. Carter sees it quite simply as the Age of Kings:

We are still in the Dark Ages, but the coronation of Charlemagne by the Pope, as Holy Roman Emperor, in the year 800 is an event of the first importance and thoroughly in accord with the Leo epoch. Indeed an age of great kings and emperors confronts us, just as, in the time of the Aries' predominance, there were the figures of the Caesars. Under the guidance of these rulers the nations of Europe, arising from the broken remnants of the old empire, take shape. Above all, the French nation begins its career appropriately under a Leo note. In England, at this time, we have Alfred the Great.

6. The sixth epoch is Virgo, the Virgin, 900–1080. It is a mutable earth sign ruled by Mercury. Virgo is the craftswoman, the critic and the healer. She is practical and particular, and rules doctors, nurses and all servers. Carter is strangely silent, finding little to say about this epoch, declaring its Virgoan traits to be 'only obscurely characterized.' He lists the Magyar conquest of Hungary, the Viking invasions and the Norman conquest of England in 1066 but without much conviction. Then, rather half-heartedly, he mentions the Seljuk Turks:

> But perhaps one may note the coming into prominence of the Seljuk Turks. Turkey is said to be ruled by Virgo and this may be a racial, not a territorial, rulership.

Now here, not for the first time, I find myself so stimulated by the striking correspondences which Carter *does* make, that I am frustrated and perplexed by those that he *does not* make. Why doesn't he see the correspondence between the Virgoan ruler Mercury and the revival of the monastic ideal during the Virgoan epoch? Is there no link between Mercury-Hermes and the archetype of the hermit? Don't monks and monasteries embody and institutionalize these hermetic qualities on a grand scale? Why does he omit the most important spiritual and cultural movement of the Epoch? Whatever the reason, the same Hermetic-Mercurial forces which swept the north European tribes to victory over the Roman Empire in the fifth century, returned in the tenth to lay the firm foundations of the Europe we know today, as a definable Christian cultural entity.

Centred at Cluny in northern France from 910, and subsequently expanding for the two centuries of the Virgoan epoch, there was a massive resurgence of monasticism spreading throughout Europe. Teaching, healing, ordering and highly disciplined, it was the embodiment of Virgoan Christian spirituality as were its principles of strict ascetic virginity and obedience. Likewise, the rise of Romanesque architecture with its fortress-like weight, solid foundations, round arches and static forms, epitomized the well-ordered virtues of this earthy practical sign. As its name implies, the Romanesque Age looked back to the Roman period and built to endure.

In addition, I find myself irritated by Carter's tentative reference to the westward expansion of the Seljuk Turks in the latter half of this period. It is not that he is wrong, quite the reverse. Had he known, he would have mentioned the historic and fateful results of that expansion in so far as it closed the pilgrim routes for Christians going to the Holy Land and also threatened Constantinople. It was these developments, which triggered the First Crusade and led to some of the main features of the next epoch of Libra.

7. The seventh epoch is Libra, the Scales, 1080–1260. This is a cardinal air sign, ruled by Venus and is associated with the scales of justice, the balance of opposites, culture and beauty. It rules all partnerships; marriages, romantic liaisons, as well as business and social relationships. In contrast to the Virgoan epoch, Carter finds Libran qualities clearly manifest in the Libran epoch:

> The Libra epoch begins about 1080 and is, in my view, very clearly shown indeed. Literature and culture revive, and we come to the age of chivalry and romance. In 1096 we have the First Crusade. Doubtless most of the Crusaders were ruffians, at least by our standards, but it is still true that their expeditions were, at any rate for the best of them, inspired by an ideal.
>
> In 1110 my conspectus mentions one of the first of the miracle plays as being performed, and in 1139 Geoffrey of Monmouth's *History of the Britons*, the basis of all the vast literature of the Arthurian romances, is in existence.
>
> The University of Salerno is said to have been founded in 1150 and the same date is given approximately for the appearance of the Teutonic epic, the *Nibelungenlied*. In 1160 Crétien de Troyes, one of the great French poets of the period of romance, flourished. The University of Paris was founded about 1210.
>
> One must not overlook Arabian scholarship. Then there were the troubadours and minnesingers, Walther von der Vogelweide flourished around the beginning of the thirteenth century. William of Lorris wrote the *Romaunt of the Rose* about 1237 which brings us to the close of the period. Fortunately the cultural seeds sown in the Libra time continue to produce their flowers into this day.

Although Carter does not give any examples of Libran seeds which are still producing their flowers, we could speculate that he might have been referring for instance to Wagner's *Ring Cycle* as a late flowering of the *Nibelunglied*, to the passion of Victorian artists for romantic depictions of Grail knights and, among other more recent retellings of the story of Arthur, to T.H. White's *The Once and Future King*.

From what we have already noted about the Epoch of Libra, all that Carter refers to as exemplifying Libran characteristics rings true. Indeed, it was such a seminal time that it is possible to add many more examples. The most arresting of these is in the rise of the Gothic cathedrals. It can be noted that there is an extraordinary synchronicity between the main publications of the Arthurian-Grail literature and the equivalent pioneering work in Gothic architecture. For instance, during the time when Geoffrey of Monmouth was writing *The Prophecies of Merlin* and his *History*, i.e. 1130–36, Sens, the first complete Gothic cathedral, was being built. During the time he was researching *The Life of Merlin*, Abbot Suger was doing his influential Gothic innovations at St. Denis in Paris (1140s), and during the time of the publications of the romances of Chrétian de Troyes, Robert de Boron and Wolfram von Eschenbach (1170–1225), Chartres cathedral was being built along with many other Gothic foundations such as Paris, Senlis and Laon.

This remarkable synchronicity seems entirely appropriate because the Arthurian-Grail literature and the Gothic cathedrals both express Libran qualities in different ways. For instance, the former, as historical romances, express the Libran association with partnerships, marriage and romance. Libra is a masculine sign but is ruled by Venus the goddess of love. This is why it rules the creative balance, or marriage, of opposites. Likewise, the Gothic cathedrals exemplify the same balance of opposites in the dynamic tension between the two arcs of the Gothic arch, and the flying buttresses and pinnacles, without which the soaring structures would have fallen apart. The stained glass and rose windows exemplify the Libran quality of beauty while the increasing height of the buildings bear witness to the physical expression of the spiritual aspiration of its cardinal air energies, reaching up to heaven. The fact that in the period of transition between Romanesque and Gothic almost all the new cathedrals were built after fires on their original Romanesque foundations, shows that the Gothic would not have been possible without the solid enduring strength and disciplined craftsmanship of the preceding epoch of Virgo.

8. The eighth epoch is that of Scorpio, the Scorpion, 1260–1440. This is a fixed water sign ruled by Mars and its new ruler is Pluto, the god of the Underworld. It is associated with death and the after-life, with survival and regeneration. It rules sex, banking, legacies, illness, vengeance, secrecy, discord, torture and the occult. Carter finds many of these qualities to be prominent during this epoch:

> Assuming that Scorpio takes over about 1260, we have the massacre of the Sicilian Vespers in 1282, and before that, in 1252, I see the ominous note that Innocent IV then approved the use of torture for the discovery of heresy. This period also covers the first use of gunpowder, a compound that was the first of so many deadly agencies.
>
> The Hundred Years War between France and England began in 1338 and ended a few years after the epoch of Scorpio. We have also endless Anglo-Scottish conflicts. Very characteristic was the Black Death which reached England in 1349 and had immense social consequences.
>
> A higher aspect of the sign is seen in the development in this age of Christian mysticism; one finds such names as Tauler, Ruysbroek, Julian of Norwich.

Once again, while not wishing to be too critical and while agreeing completely with Carter as far as he goes, it is still disappointing that he makes no mention of church developments except for the mystics. For instance, this was the epoch, which saw the rise in the Sale of Indulgences granting time off Purgatory, the building of oratories and chantries where prayers were said for the dead, the traffic in relics and the increasing corruption which surrounded these Scorpionic characteristics.

9. The ninth epoch is that of Sagittarius, the Archer, 1440–1620. This is a mutable fire sign ruled by Jupiter. It is associated with higher education, religion and long-distance travel. Its characteristics are mental energy, optimism and over-indulgence. This epoch covers the Italian Renaissance, the Reformation and the worldwide expansion of Europe, so Carter finds it easy to identify these Sagittarian developments:

> The first item on my conspectus is 1440 itself, and under it the entry: Invention of Printing with movable types by Coster at Haarlem. It was not until 1475 that the first book was printed in the English language.

In 1453 Constantinople fell to the Turks and as a consequence Greek refugees spread the ancient culture of their race over the west.

The Western Hemisphere was opened up by Columbus in 1492 and a long list of dates of eminent geographical discoveries and feats of exploration could easily be compiled, were this necessary. However, these achievements are common knowledge: what must be stressed is that the dominant power, and the one most active in opening up and subduing the New World, is that of Spain — a Sagittarian country.

Moreover, much of the period is known to us as the Elizabethan Age, and it is probable that that monarch was the outstanding figure of the whole age. Her correct ascendant is Capricorn, but she had Jupiter in Sagittarius.

It would be natural to expect religion to play a great part in a Sagittarian epoch; and so indeed it does. Martin Luther published his theses at Wittenberg in 1517 and the Reformation rapidly gathered strength. This again is common knowledge and there is no need to dwell upon the subject, which nevertheless is as characteristic of the ninth sign as is the spirit of exploration and adventure.

Carter goes on to identify the Sagittarian signature in the cult of the beard and of the padded doublets at the end of this epoch. These exaggerated the parts of the body ruled by Sagittarius! He also notes that Jupiter the ruler of this epoch was probably behind the Peasants' Revolt in Germany in 1524 and the founding of the Jesuits in 1539. He also claims that the early experiments in natural science were Jupitarian:

There are also the beginnings of natural science in the modern sense. In 1589 Galileo was dropping cannon balls from the leaning tower of Pisa to disprove the Aristotelian doctrine that the speed of falling bodies is determined by their weight. Soon after he was using the telescope — a typically Jovian instrument — and the wonders of the heavens were being revealed in a manner hitherto undreamed of. Copernicus' *De Revolutionibus* had been printed some forty-six years earlier. Kepler began publishing in 1609, towards the end of this epoch.

10. The tenth epoch is that of Capricorn, the Goat, 1620–1800. This is a cardinal earth sign ruled by Saturn. It is the sign of the statesman, the ambassador and the scientist. Its characteristics are authority, ambition and status. It rules empire, the civil service and rank. Carter sees it plainly stamped on this epoch in the rise of the European Empires, based on the explorations of the world under the previous epoch. He believes the literary and architectural classicism of the period has a strong Saturnian connection as does the Puritan revolutions of the seventeenth century. He puts these and the Thirty Years war in Germany down to the influence of Mars, which is exalted in Capricorn. Likewise, the firm establishment of modern science, beginning with Bacon's *Novum Organum* in 1620, is attributable to painstaking Capricornian analysis. He finds the founding of the Bank of England in 1694 a very Saturnian event, as is the industrial development of the iron industry and inventions such as the steam engine.

11. The eleventh epoch is that of Aquarius, the Water Carrier or Water Pourer, 1800–1980. This is a fixed air sign whose old ruler like Capricorn is Saturn but whose new ruler is Uranus, which was only discovered in 1781. Following the astrological belief that after a new planet is discovered its influence is widely felt and its attributes can be discerned in contemporary events, Carter believes that the epoch of Aquarius was hastened by the discovery of Uranus, who was quickly assigned to be its new ruler. Thus, apart from its old ruler Saturn and the characteristics associated with the tenth house as listed above, Aquarius is believed to carry the new attributes of Uranus, namely unpredictable revolution, eccentricity and bohemian genius. In a word it is associated with 'the new' and of course is the planet of the coming new age of Aquarius. The eleventh sign is the sign of friendship, humanitarian and community spirit, of liberty, equality and fraternity, of science and astrology — for the ruler of astrology is Urania. Carter finds the attributes of Aquarius written large over this epoch:

> But the advent of Aquarius is hastened, or at least complicated, by the discovery of Uranus in the year 1781. Already in 1776 there had been the American Declaration of Independence and this was virtually carried into effect by 1781, when Lord Cornwallis surrendered to a Franco-American army at Georgetown.

But the Capricorn 'influence' lasted well. That very Saturnian work, *The Decline and Fall of the Roman Empire*, was first published in 1776, and so also was Adam Smith's *Wealth of Nations*. James Watt patented his steam engine in 1782, and as the epoch ended we come to a veritable revolution, or spate of revolutions, in literature, economic life and politics. Once again there is no need to particularize but, as regards literature, it may be observed that Johnson died and Burns' first volume of poems was printed in the same year, 1786.

Louis XVI was executed in 1793. Thomas Paine's *Rights of Man*, a most Aquarian work, had appeared two years earlier.

So we come to the beginning of an Aquarian epoch in 1800. Not the Aquarian Age ... Of this Aquarian epoch which began in 1800 or thereabouts and will persist until 1980, we know enough without there being any need whatever to examine its trends in detail ... An incredible development of natural science has occurred and there has been a movement towards economic equality and the ideals of humanism, horribly interrupted, it is true, in our own day. This interruption we would like to ascribe to the entry into the human consciousness of the planet Pluto, the bringer to light of that which lies hidden. When humanity has adjusted itself to that fresh value, the present collapse of international morality may pass away and give place to something more ideal than Europe has previously known.

This last point refers to the effect of the discovery of Pluto in 1930 and its manifestation in the contemporary rise of fascism through Europe, as embodied in the dictators Franco, Mussolini and above all Hitler.

Carter died before the epoch of Aquarius ended in 1980 and so can hardly be accused of not doing justice to the eleventh house, particularly in a short essay which was probably originally given as only one lecture. However, once again it must be said that it is disappointing that he did not mention the concept of the 'Avant Garde' in the arts and in culture generally. From the 1870s onwards, this became *the* major theme right through to the excesses of the 1970s, and is still very much with us today. The 'shock of the New' leading to novelty and eccentricity for its own sake, is surely very much an excessive expression of Aquarius' new ruler Uranus.

12. The twelfth epoch is that of Pisces, the Fishes, 1980–2160. This is a mutable water sign, whose old ruler is Jupiter and whose new ruler is Neptune. It is the sign of the dreamer, the mystic and the suffering servant. Its characteristics are humility, sacrificial service and loss. It is associated with enclosures, cloisters, hospitals, prisons and all those who work in them. Carter did not live to see the transition from the Aquarian to the Piscean epoch, so I will attempt to do so for him. In the spirit in which he identified major synchronicities between the sign and the epoch, I will do likewise.

The first thing I notice is that the term 'Post-Modernism' began to be used, eclipsing the earlier notion of 'Late Modernism,' around 1980; in other words, on cue. Post Modernism, under the influence of Neptune, the new ruler of Pisces, started to dissolve the rigid mechanistic structures set up by Saturn during the previous 360 years. This has been especially noticeable in the overthrow of the collectivist tyranny of Communism and the dogmatism of socialism, which has been replaced by the more flexible concept of the mixed economy. This trend has been equally noticeable in the growth of relativism and pluralism in philosophical and religious fields.

Pisces is a feminine sign and as such I would ascribe the Women's movement to her and to her opposite, yet complementary, sign Virgo. Together, I believe, they have also been responsible for the Green movement and for the growth of general awareness that the earth's resources should no longer be regarded merely as commodities but as integral parts of a living holistic ecosystem personified by the earth goddess, Gaia.

Pisces is the mystic and the dreamer as mentioned, and it is truly remarkable that, if we look back to the Piscean epoch of the last Cosmic Age, that is, to the 180 years before the birth of Jesus Christ, we find the emergence of similar mystical characteristics. After two centuries of scepticism and rationalism, very like those which we have recently passed through, which we have associated with the epochs of Capricorn and Aquarius, there was a revival of very Piscean attributes in the resurgence of the ancient Mystery religions, especially in their belief in revelation through dreams. Martin Hengel, in *Judaism and Hellenism*, describes the spirit of those times, of which the Essenes were a notable example:

> The revival of piety after the collapse of traditional forms of religion in the *polis* and the wave of destructive scepticism in

the fourth and third centuries BC, have as a typical feature the personal tie of the individual to particular deities, a tie which was grounded more strongly than in the earlier period through personal supernatural experiences, dreams, epiphanies, healings, direct instructions from God, etc.[2]

This could be a description of what is happening today! The long wave of destructive scepticism since eighteenth century rationalism, has undermined the traditional churches, whose membership has declined drastically. On the other hand the growth of interest in alternative spiritual paths and what might loosely be called New Age Consciousness, in which experience of dreams has been central since the time of Freud and especially Jung, has been very great. Epiphanies, associated with the experiences of spiritual gifts in Pentecostal and Charismatic Churches, and in the counter-culture with shamanism, have also been considerable. Likewise the development of healing 'miracles' through complementary medicines and the awareness of divine entities through channelling and out-of-body experiences, have all contributed to an enormous rise in mystical consciousness, which is very new and very Neptunian.

From all these developments, I would list the three main characteristics which have emerged during the first twenty-five years of the Piscean epoch as, first, pluralism; second, mystical experiences, and third, its negative counterfeit — the destructive, experiences caused by drug abuse, religious fundamentalism or terrorism. This third characteristic is so well known that, as Carter would say, it does not need to be detailed, yet perhaps it is important to stress that if the mystical and esoteric aspects of the monotheistic religions, had not been either marginalized, condemned as heresy or laughed at by mainstream orthodoxy in religion and science over so many centuries, it might have been possible to introduce our younger generations to the real experience of mystical spirituality which they crave instead of allowing the counterfeit to destroy them. This may be where Christian astrology could help. This may be where the study of the stars and of ancient star-lore could bring hope. This may be where the identification of cosmic pattern amidst the apparent random flux of life could bring a sense of purpose.

Can we recognize a pattern in the outline of European history as Charles Carter has defined it? Is it convincing or is it merely his own subjective selection of facts, which he has imposed on a meaningless plethora of historical data? The only way this question can be answered is whether his selection of facts is convincing. Is his essay on the twelve epochs of the Piscean Age worthy of serious examination and possible approval?

For myself, and here it has to be personal, I am convinced not only by the immense amount of major historical events and movements which seem to fit Carter's pattern but also by the great number of equally important events which I have been annoyed that he has left out, but which I have been able to add! I would go further and claim that he has identified the outline of a harmonic pattern of cosmic time equivalent to that which was outlined with regard to cosmic space. He has shown that despite the profound scepticism with which patterns of history are generally regarded, it is possible to discern just such a pattern, which might well bear closer scrutiny, and help us to feel part of the continuously unfolding purpose of God from the past to the future.

12. The Future: Pisces and Aquarius

Having now almost completed these investigations, it would seem to be appropriate to say a little more about the characteristics of the present times, other than those already mentioned above as being typical of the new Piscean Epoch. However, before I do so, I would like to explain how it has come about that we have ended our outline of Charles Carter's Epochs with the Epoch of Pisces, whereas in earlier chapters, the main point made was that we were moving out of Pisces into Aquarius! How can this paradox be resolved?

It is easy to resolve this apparent paradox once we remember that in the earlier chapters, it was stressed that we were moving from the *Age* of Pisces into the *Age* of Aquarius. Both of these were Ages or Months of the Great Year of 25,920 years (see Chapter 6). The Great Year, it was explained, consisted of twelve Ages or Months each of 2,160 years which, because of the backward movement of what is called 'the precession of the equinoxes,' goes in the opposite direction to the annual zodiac. Thus the Ages of the Great Year move from Pisces to Aquarius. However, the twelve *Epochs*, which we have just been outlining, are all 180-year subdivisions of the Age of Pisces and according to Carter move in the same direction as the zodiac. This explains the paradox. It also explains why, as mentioned earlier, most astrologers do not like to make use of the Ages of the Great Year. They believe they are far too vague and inexact to explain the details of any historical process and might even be used to imply the opposite of what proved to be the case! Not that this could ever be entirely so. What was said in earlier chapters about the New Age still stands, although much that was thought to have been heralding its coming has now been seen to have been attributable to the *Epoch* of Aquarius which we have identified to have been between 1800 and 1980. A good analogy can be taken from the hour and minute hand of a clock. The Ages are like the hours while the Epochs are like the minutes. However, this analogy should not be pressed too far, otherwise the hands would have to appear to be going in the opposite directions!

Richard Tarnas, author of *The Passion of the Western Mind*, and a leading astrologer, has found a way of synthesizing the movement of the Ages from Pisces to Aquarius with that of the Epochs from Aquarius to Pisces. He does so by looking at the conjunction of Neptune and Uranus, the new rulers of Pisces and Aquarius respectively. This took place in 1993, but is still affecting us all collectively. He says that Neptune dissolves structures like salt water corroding the iron girders of Brighton Pier. Uranus, on the other hand, brings sudden revolution as it did in the American, French and Russian revolutions. He puts these two attributes together to create the concept 'Revolution by dissolution' and claims that because of the joint power of these two outer planets, 'revolution by dissolution' is the chief characteristic of the present times.

In an essay called *Prometheus the Awakener* Tarnas says that the revolutionary action of Uranus is similar to that attributed to Prometheus in classical mythology. He outlines the enormous range of the contemporary 'revolution by dissolution,' amplifying as he does so, the key themes already mentioned, namely pluralism, mysticism and drugs:

> The Uranus-Neptune combination is associated, both in history and in personal biographies, with periods in which the archetypal — the mythic, the spiritual, the transcendent, the imaginal, the numinous — is suddenly awakened and liberated in new ways into human consciousness. We see this all around us now: the tremendous upswelling of interest today in an astonishing multiplicity of spiritual paths and traditions, in esoteric disciplines, in the transpersonal movement, in meditation and mystical religious traditions, in Jungian and archetypal psychology, in mythology and ancient religions, in shamanism and indigenous traditions, in the recovery of Goddess spirituality and the feminine dimension of the divine, in eco-feminism spirituality, in psychedelic self-exploration and new forms of experiential psychotherapy that effect profound changes of consciousness, in the emergence of holistic paradigms in every field, in the desire to merge with a great unity — to reconnect with the Earth and all forms of life on it, with the cosmos, with the community of being, We see it in the powerful new awareness of the *anima mundi*, the soul of the world. And we see it in the widespread urge to overcome old separatisms and dualisms — between human beings and nature, between spirit and matter, mind and

body, subject and object, intellect and soul, and perhaps most fundamentally, between masculine and feminine — to discover a deeper unitive consciousness.[1]

Tarnas goes on to draw a parallel between the development of epistemological 'deconstruction' which has taken place in 'postmodernity' since the beginning of the 1980s and the rise of perestroika and glasnost under Gorbachev which led to the eventual dissolution of the Soviet Union, The latter took place in 1989–1990 when Jupiter came into opposition with the Uranus-Neptune conjunction. He says that the liberation of millions of people from the oppression of Communism and the Cold War and the spread of the democratic ideal round the world after this, were the most spectacular results of this conjunction.

However, there has been a downside to this Uranus-Neptune 'revolution by dissolution,' the most obvious of which, as mentioned earlier, have been drug abuse and terrorism. But there are many other negative examples, of which we need also to be aware:

Of course every archetypal combination has its shadow side, and the Uranus-Neptune conjunction is no exception. The collective psyche's highly activated thirst for transcendence, while ultimately spiritual in nature, has brought forth a wide range of less exalted impulses and behaviours. The collective impulse towards escapism and denial, passivity and narcissism, credulity and delusion, the hyperstimulating rapidity of technologically produced images signifying nothing, the hypnotic fascination with and addition to image ('image is everything'), indeed the widespread obsession with addiction of all kinds — from drugs and alcohol to consumerism and television — these and many more forms of accelerated and intensified maya make less unambiguous the positive virtues of such other characteristic Uranus-Neptune phenomena as interactive electronic multimedia and 'virtual reality.' (We see suggestive signs of a disruptively hyperactivated Neptune on more literal levels as well, with massive floods, tidal waves, disasters at sea, oil spills, industrial accidents involving liquids and gases.) The intensified religious consciousness of the age has given rise to cult movements, fundamentalist fanaticism, and a host of eccentric 'new age' infatuations. The dissolving of rigid structures in the psyche permitting the emergence of non-ordinary states of consciousness and genuine mystical illumination, but leading to destructively delusory states as well. Seldom has the need for discernment been more critical.[2]

Richard Tarnas has said enough to confirm that, although we have only been in the Epoch of Pisces since 1980, there are nevertheless many signs that indicate that we are indeed in the Epoch of the twelfth sign of the zodiac. What then of the future? Detailed prediction would not be appropriate for a study of this kind except to say of course that because we have only been in this Epoch for a quarter century and it will last for 180 years, we may reasonably expect much, much more of the same!

Nevertheless, despite a reluctance to stray into the future, some further indications may be made by attempting to identify the Epoch with a particular name of an individual apostle. There are many New Testament texts which imply that there were twelve Apostles because there are twelve signs of the zodiac, not least, in the details of the New Jerusalem which featured so prominently in earlier chapters. In Chapter 1 'The New Jerusalem and the Cosmos,' it was demonstrated that the twelve jewels, which adorned its foundations were symbolic of the twelve signs of the zodiac. These began with jasper or diamond, which symbolized Aries, which we identified with the impetuous yet fickle Peter in a later chapter. However, it is not so easy to ascribe the individual names of other Apostles to any of the other signs or Epochs. We are told in Revelation 21, verse 14 that the wall of the New Jerusalem 'had twelve foundations and on them the twelve names of the twelve apostles of the Lamb,' but we are not told in what order those names appeared! In the gospels themselves, the apostles are listed several times but not exactly in the same order, so it would appear to be unwise to speculate further unless some other system of allocation could be found.

One other such system could perhaps be found when we remember that the so-called Four Evangelists or gospel writers have been allocated the symbols of the 'four living creatures' from Revelation and Ezekiel since earliest times. These feature large on the timpani of Romanesque and Gothic cathedrals round the central figure of Christ. They are: the man who is Matthew, the bull who is Luke, the lion who is Mark and the eagle who is John. These 'four living creatures' are in fact symbolic of the four fixed signs of the zodiac, i.e. Aquarius the man, Taurus the bull, Leo the lion and Scorpio whose exalted sign is the eagle. Although neither Mark nor Luke were Apostles, it would at least make an uncontroversial allocation to start with. It would also upstage any anxious quest for the Epoch of Judas, which might be invidious to say the least, or the Epoch of Matthias who replaced him (Acts 1:29) which might be boring, because like Thaddeus he never appears again!

If we accept the gospel writers as those who, through their writing, represent all the apostles, this would chime with the ancient belief that the four fixed signs somehow represented the whole zodiac. The implication of this is easy to understand: while there are indeed twelve signs, there are only four elements, i.e. fire, air, water and earth. Each of the four fixed signs is taken from a different element, Taurus is earth, Leo is fire, Scorpio is water and Aquarius is air. They are thus representative of all four elements which together make up the twelve because there are three signs in each element, one cardinal, one fixed and one mutable. If we were to assume that each of the fixed signs also represented the other two signs in each element, then we could say that Taurus represented the other earth signs, i.e. Virgo and Capricorn, Leo the other fire signs, Aries and Sagittarius, Scorpio the other water signs Cancer and Pisces, and Aquarius the other air signs Gemini and Libra. Many astrologers do in fact hold that all the signs in the same element are closely linked by their common element and therefore it would be true in this sense

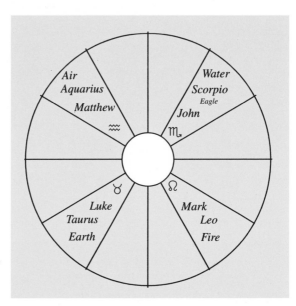

Fig.12.1. The four fixed signs of the zodiac and the four gospel writers.

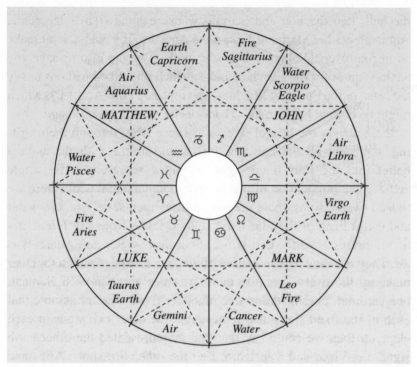

Fig.12.2. The four fixed signs and their relation to the other two signs in each element.

to say that the Epoch of Pisces was ruled or was part of the threefold water triplicity symbolized by Scorpio and the Eagle of St John and which also included Cancer.

In astrology the three signs in each element are not only linked by their shared element but also by an angle of 120 degrees which is called a Trine. This is the most beneficent 'aspect' in astrology and is associated with all that is harmonious. Measured against Charles Carter's epochs, 120 degrees is four signs each of 30 degrees. This means that a Trine is equal to 720 years. If we go back 720 years we come to the late thirteenth century. What is remarkable is that that period, the early years of the Epoch of Scorpio, is associated with some very famous mystics such as Julian of Norwich, Meister Eckhart, Tauler and Ruysbroek. There were hard times as well in those days, associated with war and plague, as indeed is ours. Nevertheless it is important to stress with Christian assurance, that just as the Epoch of Scorpio, despite its many problems, gave good testimony to the inspiration of St John and his mystical gospel, so the Epoch of Pisces, despite the

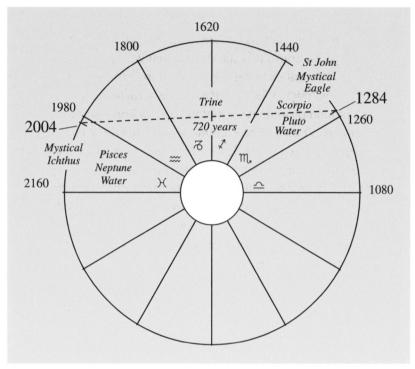

Fig.12.3. The Trine of 720 years.

many problems which will continue to plague it such as those already mentioned above, will also give a good testimony to the mystical power of Jesus himself. For we must not forget that Pisces is Ichthus the Great Fish, who does not drown but comes walking on the water in the darkest eye of the storm. It is Ichthus who can transform the worst of times into the best of times. We must also remember that, although we are moving towards the Age of Aquarius, we still have over one hundred years of the Age of Pisces left to go. So we are in fact still in the Age and the Epoch of Pisces. There's going to be a lot of mystical experience and delusory illusion still to go! There's going to be an awful lot more water around, which may endanger us all through global warming and global dimming.

To finish on a positive note, it is important to reaffirm the close link between Neptune and Uranus at this time, made by Richard Tarnas. The Trine in water signs between Pisces and Scorpio is real enough but that is looking back. Looking forward, we can see that although the Epoch of Aquarius is over, the dawn rays of the Age of Aquarius can already be seen. Aquarius, as said earlier, is the water pourer and the water he pours is not more literal water to flood us still further (see Chapter 9). His water is of the spirit. It is the spirit of Ichthus, which he pours out on all flesh. This is already happening in all the positive indications of the spiritual revolution, which Tarnas enumerated. As we move through the Epoch of Ichthus we move out of the Age of Ichthus into the Age of the Spirit Pourer. This will be exciting. We will not drown in the waters but be carried up into the air. The wind of the spirit will transform the Scorpion into the Dove symbolizing the abating of the flood and into the Eagle of St John who will bear us on his powerful wings through all the crystal spheres of the microcosm to the macrocosm and the nearer presence of God. What a journey! One which we have already taken in our minds throughout this study but which then we will experience in all its fullness.

Endnotes

Introduction

1. 'The White Train' *The Observer Colour Supplement*, London, 7 October 1984.
2. Northcott, Michael, *An Angel Directs the Storm.*
3. Northcott, *An Angel Directs the Storm*, p. 67.
4. Northcott, *An Angel Directs the Storm*, p. 3.
5. Brown, Dan, *The Da Vinci Code*, p. 268.
6. Brown, Dan, *The Da Vinci Code*, p. 268.
7. See Butler, Christopher, *Number Symbolism*, p. 24.

Chapter 1

1. Norman Cohn, *The Pursuit of the Millennium.*
2. Adrian Gilbert, *The New Jerusalem*, p. 324.
3. John Michell, *City of Revelation.*
4. John F. Walvoord, *The Revelation of Jesus Christ*, p. 323: 'It also could be in the form of a pyramid with sides sloping to a peak at the height indicated ... This would have certain advantages ... because this shape provides a vehicle for the river of life to proceed out of the throne of God, which seems to be at the top, to find its way to the bottom, assuming our experience of gravity will be somewhat normal also in the new earth.' See also W.H. Simcox, *The Revelation*, p. 136 for similar practical considerations!

5. See F.F. Bruce, *A New Testament Commentary*, p. 664.
6. *Sibylline Oracles* V, line 251 (AD 88–130).
7. E.g. Henry Barclay Swete, *The Apocalypse of St John*, p. 289; Martin Kiddle, *The Revelation of St John*, p. 430.
8. Lewis Mumford, *The City in History*, p. 31. For a detailed expression of Mumford's position, with special reference to ancient Mesopotamia, see Thorkild Jacobson (with Frankfort and others) *Before Philosophy,* Chapter 5, 'Mesopotamia: the cosmos as a state.'
9. Lewis Mumford, p. 49.
10. E.g. Philip Carrington, *The Meaning of the Revelation*, p. 346; Austin Farrar, *The Revelation of St John the Divine,* p. 218; Edward Schick, *The Revelation of St John*, Vol 2, p. 105; Thomas Kelper, *The Book of Revelation*, p. 213.
11. E.g. Isbon T. Beckwith, *The Apocalypse of John*, p. 760; G.E. Ladd, *A Commentary on the Revelation of John*, p. 282.
12. M.R. Newbolt, *The Book of Unveiling*, p. 197.
13. Otto Neugebauer, *The Exact Sciences in Antiquity*, pp. 93 and 36 respectively.
14. Plato, *Timaeus*, section 22.
15. Plato, *Timaeus*, section 23.
16. Plato, *Timaeus*, section 22.
17. Gyorgy Doczi, *The Power of Limits: proportional harmonies in nature, art and architecture.*
18. *Sefer Yesira,* paragraph 47. See Peter Hayman 'Some

observations on Sefer Yesira (1). Its Use of Scripture,' *Journal of Jewish Studies* Vol XXXV No.2, Autumn 1984, Oxford p. 176. Hayman's observations are based on Professor I. Gruenwald's 'Preliminary Critical Edition of Sefer Yesira,' *Israel Oriental Studies*, I, 1971, p. 163. Gruenwald's edition is of the hitherto neglected long recension in the oldest extant manuscript of the book: *Vatican (Cat. Assemani)* 299 (8), fols 66a–71b. Some scholars argue a later date for this document.

19. Carl Sagan, *Cosmos*, p. 264.
20. For exceptions to this see G.R. Beasley-Murray, *Revelation*, p. 325n.
21. Athanasius Kircher, *Oedipus Aegyptiacus*, II, ii 177 ff, 1653.
22. R.H. Charles, *The Revelation of St John*.
23. E.g. Martin Kiddle, *The Revelation of St John*, p. 434.
24. E.g. Ronald H. Preston and Anthony Hanson, *The Revelation of St John the Divine*, p. 132; G.B. Caird, *The Revelation of St John the Divine*, p. 277.
25. Leon Morris, *The Revelation of St John*, p. 252.
26. G.R. Beasley-Murray, *Revelation*, p. 325.
27. G.R. Beasley-Murray, *Revelation*, p. 323
28. Austin Farrar, *A Rebirth of Images*, p. 216
29. J. Massyngberde Ford, *Revelation*, p. 343.
30. J.C. Cooper, *An Illustrated Encyclopaedia of Traditional Symbols*, p. 198.
31. R.H. Charles, *The Revelation of St John*. p. 170.
32. Rabbi Johanan, *Sanhedrin* 100a and Baba bathra 75; e.g. H.B. Swete, *The Apocalypse of St John*, p. 294; M. Kiddle, *The Revelation*

of St John, p. 435; L. Morris, *The Revelation of St John*, p. 253.
33. R.H. Charles, *The Apocrypha and Pseudepigraphia of the Old Testament*, Vol II, p. 237.
34. William Barclay, *The Revelation of St John*, Vol 2, p. 214.
35. J.C. Cooper, *An Illustrated Encyclopaedia of Traditional Symbols*, p. 128.
36. G.R. Beasley-Murray, *Revelation,* 326.
37. William Barclay, *The Revelation of St John*, p. 326.
38. Robert Bauval and Adrian Gilbert, *The Orion Mystery*, p. 121.
39. Adrian Gilbert, *Signs in the Sky*, p. 218.
40. E.g. the sixteenth-century paraphrase of St Augustine's hymn 'Jerusalem, my Happy Home,' *The English Hymnal*, No. 638:

Thy turrets and thy pinnacles
With carbuncles do shine;
Thy very streets are paved with gold,
Surpassing clear and fine;

Thy houses are of ivory,
Thy windows crystal clear;
Thy tiles are made of beaten gold —
O God that I were there!

See also St Bernard's 'Jerusalem the Golden,' *The English Hymnal* 412 for 'halls of Zion' and Samuel Johnson's 'City of God' *The English Hymnal* 375, for watchfires gleaming and towers arising.
41. *Plateia* could possibly be generic for 'streets' as in Rev. 11:8; cf. G.B. Caird, *The Revelation of St John the Divine*, p. 278.
42. e.g. Charles A. Sorrell and George F. Sandstrom, *The Rocks and Minerals of the World*, p. 38 'Crystal Systems: Cubic Systems.'
43. Mellie Uyldert, *The Magic of Precious Stones*, 1981.

44. Ra Bonewitz, *Cosmic Crystals*, p. 10.
45. Francis Hitching, *The World Atlas of Mysteries*, pp. 56f.
46. Plato, *Phaedo*, sections 109a–110d.
47. Ra Bonewitz, *Cosmic Crystals*, p. 130.

Chapter 2

1. For an alternative interpretation of the sacred geometry of New Jerusalem, see John Michell, *City of Revelation*. His brilliant study is, however, very difficult for those not acquainted with the gematria (the numerical correspondences to the Hebrew and Greek alphabets; it is from this that we get the word geometry) upon which his whole exposition is based. I offer my simpler version for those who know nothing of gematria or numerology. Cf. Oscar Cullmann, *Christ and Time*, p. 188, for a similar model.
2. Robert Lawlor, *Sacred Geometry, Philosophy and Practice*, pp. 4f.
3. For a comprehensive summary of the literature attributed to Hermes Trismegistus see C.H. Dodd, *The Interpretation of the Fourth Gospel*, Chapter 2: 'The person so called was represented as a sage of ancient Egypt, deified after his death as the Egyptian Hermes, that is, the god Thoth.'
4. For a full explanation of this see F.F. Bruce's standard work, *The Spreading Flame*, p. 294.
5. T.S. Eliot, *Collected Poems*, p. 191.
6. J.C. Cooper, *An Illustrated Encyclopaedia of Traditional Symbols*, p. 180.
7. Ros Herman, 'Electrons get to the heart of the matter,' *New Scientist*, 17 January, 1980.

Chapter 3

1. Leon Morris, *The Revelation of St John*, p. 250.
2. T.F. Glasson, *The Revelation of St John*, p. 118.
3. Nigel Pennick, *Sacred Geometry*, p. 60.
4. Nigel Pennick, *Sacred Geometry*, p. 118.
5. Percy Scholes, *The Concise Oxford Dictionary of Music*, p. 5.
6. Guy Murchie, *Music of the Spheres*, p. 362.
7. The extent to which these terms were part of the vocabulary of the early Church is shown, for instance, in Tatians' 'Harmony of the Four Gospels' known as the Diatessaron.
8. For a general introduction to classical architecture as frozen music see Claude Bragdon, *The Beautiful Necessity, Architecture as 'Frozen Music.'*
9. Brian Greene, *The Elegant Universe*, p. 144
10. C.F. Burney, *The Books of Kings*, p. 77.
11. James A. Montgomery, *The Books of Kings*, p. 1158.
12. John Gray, *I and II Kings*, p. 173.
13. James A. Montgomery, *The Books of Kings*, p. 152: 'The shrine of the sanctuary is a cube of 20 cubits; for such proportion cf. the Meccan Ka'ba (i.e. 'dice cube'), which is $112 \times 12m$ square, 15m high.' This is hardly relevant let alone illuminating but better than all the rest who are more concerned with the gold-plating.
14. J.C. Cooper, *An Illustrated Encyclopaedia of Traditional Symbols*, p. 116.
15. Robert Lawlor, *Sacred Geometry*, p. 58.

16. See *Enclyclopaedia Judaica*, 1971, Vol 7, p. 379 for full explanation of *gematria viz*: 'It consists of explaining a word or group of words according to the numerical value of the letters ...' etc.; 'The use of letters to signify numbers ...' etc. It was practised widely throughout the ancient world. Thus in Greek alpha = 1, beta = 2 and in Hebrew aleph = 1, beth = 2, etc.

17. John Michell, *City of Revelation*, pp. 74–75.

18. E.g. Alfred Edersheim, *The Temple, Its Ministry and Services*, pp. 186–87.

19. Roger Cook, *The Tree of Life*, p. 119: 'The sap of the tree becomes the precious 'oil of life' that burns in fruit and flower.' Cf. S.T. Coleridge's description of paradise as an oriental idyll 'Where blossomed many an incense-bearing tree.' For an excellent discussion of Eden in relation to Xanadu, see E.S. Shaffer, *Kubla Khan and the Fall of Jerusalem*, pp. 96ff.

20. J. Robinson, *The First Book of Kings*, p. 81: 'This custom was in origin a cereal offering.'

21. Roger Cook, *The Tree of Life*, p. 119: In Judaism, the Tree of Life is most often represented by the flowering almond tree, the tree which, in the Near East, heralds and hastens the spring, its radiant white blossoms appearing long before its leaves.' See also L. Yardin, *The Tree of Light*, p. 40.

22. *Encyclopaedia Judaica*, 1971, Vol 15., p. 950.

23. John Gray, *I and II Kings*, p. 171.

24. John Gray, *I and II Kings*, p. 171.

25. J.C. Cooper, *An Illustrated Encyclopaedia of Traditional Symbols*, p. 125: 'Palm; *Arabian*: the Tree of Life.'

26. C.F.D. Moule, *The Origin of Christology*, p. 90.

27. John Bowker, *Jesus and the Pharisees*, p. 49.

28. E.g. Jacob at Bethel, *Gen.*28:16–17 and Solomon's dedicatory prayer 1 *Kings* 8:27.

29. F.F. Bruch, *The Acts of the Apostles*, p. 177.

30. Bertil Gartner, *The Areaopagus Speech and Natural Revelation*, 1955, p. 251. He concludes that the passage is Pauline and that other references indicate that the Gentiles have not lacked testimony to God as 'the God Who is the Creator and Preserver of the created world.'

Chapter 4

1. Maurice Farbridge, *Studies in Biblical and Semitic Symbolism*, p. 119.

2. Ethelbert W. Bullinger, *Number in Scripture*, p. 158.

3. G.A.F. Knight, *Leviticus*, p. 152: 'Seven is the holy number.'

4. J.R. Porter, *Leviticus*, p. 38: 'Seven appears as a sacred number in the Old Testament and also throughout the ancient Near East.'

5. Ethelbert Bullinger, *Number in Scripture*, p. 158, who calls seven 'the great number in *spiritual perfection* '.

6. Maurice Farbridge, *Studies in Biblical and Semitic Symbolism*, p. 135.

7. Maurice Farbridge, *Studies in Biblical and Semitic Symbolism*, p. 135.

8. Maurice Farbridge, *Studies in Biblical and Semitic Symbolism*, p. 135.

9. J.C. Cooper, *An Illustrated Encyclopaedia of Traditional Symbols*, pp. 106f.

10. See John Michell, *City of Revelation*, 1973, p. 65: 'the number seven is rarely apparent

in physical nature, corresponding rather to the spiritual forces that regulate the cycles of time and human development.'

11. See Ernest McClain, *The Myth of Invariance*, Chapter 10 'Babylon and Sumer,' section on sexagesimal arithmetic, pp. 131–41.

12. For a detailed comparison between Leviticus and earlier calendars, especially Deuteronomy 16, see Martin Noth, *Leviticus*, pp. 165–76.

13. Scholars have been divided as to what the literal Hebrew 'from the morrow of the sabbath' means. For a summary of traditional opinions see N.H. Snaith, *Leviticus and Numbers,* p. 153.

14. N.H. Snaith, *Leviticus and Numbers,* p. 155, points out that this was also 'the ecclesiastical New Year, since in pre-exilic times the new year began with the autumn festival.'

15. N.H. Snaith, *Leviticus and Numbers,* p. 163.

16. For a graphic and ecological summary of Tabernacles see G.S.F. Knight, *Leviticus,* p. 144f.

17. Scholars are divided on whether the Jubilee was the forty-ninth or the fiftieth year. For a full discussion of the views of L.B. Paton, H. Strack, J. and H. Lewy, E. Stone, E.R. Leach, Zeililin, Klostermann, North, Kugler and others, see Donald Wilford Blosser, *Jesus and the Jubilee*, unpublished Ph.D. thesis, St Andrews University, St Mary's College Library 1979, pp. 13–17.

18. Alfred Sendrey, *Music in Ancient Israel*, p. 371.

19. J.R. Porter, *Leviticus*, p. 184, cf. G.A.F. Knight, *Leviticus*, p. 152: 'The figures seven times seven thus represent the ultimate in holiness.'

20. Robert Graves, *The White Goddess*, Chapter 15 'The Seven Pillars' pp. 259–71. See also Desmond Varley, *Seven: the Number of Creation*, pp. 1–28.

21. Geoffrey Ashe, *The Ancient Wisdom*, pp. 120–26.

22. For a wealth of comparative material on this theme see Richard J. Clifford, *The Cosmic Mountain in Canaan and the Old Testament*.

23. Percy Scholes, *The Oxford Companion to Music*, p. 591. He describes the monochord as 'nothing but a sound-box over which is stretched a single string which can be divided at any point by a movable bridge, the position of which can be accurately determined by a scale of measurements marked on the surface over which it moves. The ratios of intervals and many others of the facts that make up the foundations of the science of acoustics were discovered by its use, and for five thousand years it gave rise to intricate mathematical calculations.'

24. Robert K.G. Temple, *The Sirius Mystery*, pp. 189f, relates the Jubilee cycle to the orbit of the star Sirius B. He argues that because Moses wrote Leviticus and was 'an initiate of Egypt,' the 50-year cycle originated with the predynastic Egyptians (the Dogons). Commenting on his belief that the Jubilee year was never kept, he says 'Obviously the Hebrews did not understand the fifty-year orbit of Sirius B which Moses ... presumably had in mind.' I believe he is stretching the evidence considerably here, which is neither obvious nor presumable.

25. Herbert Whone, *The Hidden Face of Music*, pp. 56f.

26. Jack Finegan, *Handbook of Biblical Chronology*, pp. 35f.

27. Jack Finegan, *Handbook of Biblical Chronology*, p. 37.

28. Ernest McClain, *The Myth of Invariance*, p. 96.

29 . Alain Daniélou, *Introduction to the Study of Musical Scales*, pp. 70–71.

30. Robert Temple , *The Crystal Sun*, p. 507

31. David Tame, *The Secret Power of Music*, p. 249.

32. David Tame, *The Secret Power of Music*, p. 250.

33. David Tame, *The Secret Power of Music*, p. 38.

34. See N.H. Snaith, *Leviticus and Numbers,* p. 156.

Chapter 5

1. E.g. Burton Scott Eastern, *The Gospel According to St Luke*, p. 156, who says that the seventy merely helped Christ 'to make the most of a short visit;' H. Balmforth, *The Gospel According to St Luke*, p. 200; Norval Geldenhuys, *Commentary on the Gospel of Luke*, p. 299, who says they were appointed solely 'to bring spiritual ministration and prepare His way in the towns and villages that he still wishes to visit during the few months before His crucifixion.'

2. E.g. Alfred Plummer, *The Gospel According to St Luke*, p. 269; W. Manson, *The Gospel of Luke*, p. 123; William Arndt, *The Gospel According to St Luke*, p. 280; W.R.F. Browning, *The Gospel According to St Luke*, p. 109; D.W. Cleverly Ford, *A Reading of St Luke's Gospel*, p. 139.

3. E.g. Alfred Plummer, *The Gospel According to St Luke*, p.269; W.R.F. Browning,*The Gospel According to St Luke*, p. 109.

4. E. Earle Ellis, *The Gospel of Luke*, pp. 153f.

5. G.H.P. Thompson, *The Gospel According to Luke*, p. 159.

6. John Martin Creed, *The Gospel According to St Luke*, p. 144.

7. E.J. Tinsley, *The Gospel According to Luke*, p. 113.

8. Bruce M. Metzger, *Historical and Literary Studies*, Chapter 7 'Seventy or Seventy-Two Disciples?,' p. 76.

9. Bruce M. Metzger, *A Textual Commentary on the Greek New Testament*, p. 151, paragraphs in square brackets by Kurt Aland.

10. I. Howard Marshall, *The Gospel of Luke*, p. 415.

11. *Encyclopaedia Judaica*, 1971, Vol 4, p. 852.

12. Giorgio de Santillana and Hertha von Dechend, *Hamlet's Mill*, p. 66: 'Hipparchus in 127 BC called it the Precession of the Equinoxes. There is good reason to assume that he actually rediscovered this, that it had been known some thousand years previously, and that on it the Archaic Year based its long-range computation of time.'

13. *Everyman's Encyclopaedia*, Dent, London 3rd edn. 1949, Vol 10, p. 630.

14. Giorgio de Santillana and Hertha von Dechend, *Hamlet's Mill*, p. 59.

15. Rodney Collin, *The Theory of Celestial Influence*, p. 245.

16. William Stirling, *The Canon*, p. 101.

17. Guy Lyon Playfair and Scott Hill, *The Cycles of Heaven*, p. 197.

18. Ernest McClain, *The Myth of Invariance*, p. 100.

19. Alain Daniélou, *Introduction to the Study of Musical Scales*, p. 68.

20. David Tame, *The Secret Power of Music*, p. 249.

21. David Tame, *The Secret Power of Music*, p. 22.

22. David Tame, *The Secret Power of Music*, p. 23.

23. Gerhard von Rad, *Genesis,* 1961, p. 47.

24. H.C.Leupold, *Exposition of Genesis,* p. 48.
25. H.C. Leupold, *Exposition of Genesis,* p. 50.
26. David Tame, *The Secret Power of Music*, pp. 232f.
27. Ernest McClain, *The Myth of Invariance*, p. 124, re Rabbi Schochet.
28. Ernest McClain, *The Myth of Invariance*, pp. 124–127.
29. David Tame, *The Secret Power of Music*, p. 22: 'Inaudible to the human ear, this Cosmic Vibration was the origin and basis of all the matter and energy in the universe. In its purest, least differentiated form, this Cosmic Sound was known to the Hindus as OM.'
30. Captain Bruce Cathie, *The Pulse of the Universe: Harmonic 288*, flyleaf.
31. David Tame, *The Secret Power of Music*, p. 249.
32. Douglas Adams, *The Hitchhiker's Guide to the Galaxy*, pp. 134–36.
33. Strangely enough the numbers 5 and 72 also link us to the variant tradition which said that the Septuagint was translated by 72 scholars *and by five*. Henry G. Meecham, *The Oldest Version of the Bible,* p. 172, says: 'One tradition assigns the work of transliteration to five men, the translation to seventy-two men, each company carrying out its task in the time of Ptolemos.' Carl Clemen, *Primitive Christianity and its Non-Jewish Sources*, p. 103, suggests that 'the seventy-two and the five were still felt to be component parts of the year of three hundred and sixty days.'

Chapter 6

1. Gerhard Kittel, (ed.), *Theological Dictionary of the New Testament*, Vol 1, pp. 198–209.
2. Gerhard Kittel, *Theological Dictionary of the New Testament*, Vol. 1, p. 204.
3. Don Cupitt, *The Sea of Faith*, p. 106. For a summary of this school 'of consistent eschatology' see chapter 4 'Going by the Book.'
4. Albert Nolan, *Jesus Before Christianity, The Gospel of Liberation*, 1.18
5. Albert Nolan, *Jesus Before Christianity, The Gospel of Liberation*, p. 90.
6. D.S. Russell, *The Jews from Alexander to Herod*, p. 140.
7. D.S. Russell, *The Jews from Alexander to Herod*, p. 140.
8. D.S. Russell, *The Jews from Alexander to Herod*, p. 141.
9. It is interesting to note that R.H. Charles says in *The Book of Jubilees*, p. 37, that Jubilees 4:17, mentioned by Russell, 'refers mainly to 1 Enoch lxxii–lxxxii.' This is 'The Book of the Courses of the Heavenly Luminaries' in which we found justification for suggesting that the gates of New Jerusalem were 'the portals of heaven,' in chapter 1. Howard Clark Kee says that this aspect of Enochic literature 'was probably influenced by Babylonian astrology, in that it lays stress on the movement of the celestial order and the divinely intended earthly order.' *The Origins of Christianity*, p. 181.
10. C.G. Jung, *Aion,* p. 89.
11. David Hughes, *The Star of Bethlehem Mystery*, p. 13.
12. David Hughes,*The Star of Bethlehem Mystery*, p. 13
13. e.g. Theodore H. Robinson, *The Gospel of Matthew*, pp. 7f; F.W. Green, *The Gospel according to Saint Matthew*, p. 31; J.C. Fenton, *The Gospel of St Matthew*, p. 46; Raymond E. Brown, *The Birth of the Messiah*, pp. 172f.

14. David Hughes, *The Star of Bethlehem Mystery*, p. 228.

15. Werner Keller, *The Bible as History*, Chapter 36 'The Star of Bethlehem,' pp. 331–39.

16. P. A.H. Seymour, *The Birth of Christ, Exloring the Myth*, p. 189. For a fascinating alternative account see Adrian Gilbert: *Magi, The Quest For a Secret Tradition*.

17. David Hughes, *The Star of Bethlehem Mystery*, p. 227.

18. Werner Keller, *The Bible as History*, p. 336.

19. Giorgio de Santillana and Hertha von Dechend, *Hamlet's Mill*, pp. 244f.

20. Giorgio de Santillana and Hertha von Dechend, *Hamlet's Mill*, p. 59.

21. David R. Cartlidge and David L. Dungan, in *Documents for the Study of the Gospels*, p. 178, refer to Virgil's *Eclogue IV* as 'A Roman 'Messianic' Prophecy' and offer the following translation:
The ultimate age of Cumae's song is now come!
The great order is born anew from the line of the ages.
The Virgin has now returned; Saturn's reign has returned;
Now a new offspring is sent from Heaven on High.
You alone grant favour at the birth of the boy by whom the iron age
Shall cease and a golden race shall rise up on the world,
Only you, chaste Lucina; now your own Apollo reigns.

22. Alan Oken, *Astrology: Evolution and Revolution*, p. 28.

23. Alan Oken, *Astrology: Evolution and Revolution*, p. 22.

24. Vera W. Reid, *Towards Aquarius*, pp. 60f.

Chapter 7

1. C.H. Dodd, *The Interpretation of the Fourth Gospel*, pp. 236ff. For his full exposition see pp. 230–38.

2. Kenneth G. Cuming, *God and the New Age*. Articles based on a course of sermons delivered at the Church of Christ the Healer, Burrswoood, p. 8.

3. See Bernard Capp, *Astrology and the Popular Press*, Chapter 5 'Almanacs and Religion' for a detailed account of the ambivalent attitude of the churches to astrology.

4. See the works of Michel and Françoise Gauquelin, *The Cosmic Clocks*, and *The Truth about Astrology*. The most authoritative assessment of the Gauquelins' work is found in H.F. Eysenck and D.K.B. Nias, *Astrology, Science or Superstition?*

5. Eric Newton and William Neil, *The Christian Faith in Art*, p. 31

6. Eric Newton and William Neil, *The Christian Faith in Art*.

7. Gilbert Cope, *Symbolism in the Bible and in the Church*, p. 37.

8. Gilbert Cope, *Symbolism in the Bible and in the Church*, p. 35.

9. Edward Hulme, *Symbolism in Christian Art*, pp. 197f.

10. Tertullian, *de Baptismo*, in Gilbert Cope, *Symbolism in the Bible and in the Church*, p. 37.

11. Gilbert Cope, *Symbolism in the Bible and in the Church*.

12. Gilbert Cope, *Symbolism in the Bible and in the Church*.

13. Herbert Whone, *Church, Monastery, Cathedral*, p. 73.

14. Herbert Whone, *Church, Monastery, Cathedral*, p. 74.

15. Herbert Whone, *Church, Monastery, Cathedral*, pp. 105f.

16. John Michell, *City of Revelation*, p. 72.

17. Robert Lawlor, *Sacred Geometry*, p. 35.

18. Herbert Whone, *Church, Monastery, Cathedral*, p. 112.
19. Robert Lawlor, *Sacred Geometry*, pp. 33–35.

Chapter 8

1. Lois Lang-Sims, *The Christian Mystery*, p. 68: 'Many people have seen in this 'water bearer' a symbol of the dawn of the Aquarian age at the expiration of the Piscean, the fish being a recognized symbol of the Christ.'
2. Peter Lemesurier, *The Gospel of the Stars*, p. 43.
3. Vera W. Reid, *Towards Aquarius*, p. 92.
4. Johannes Behm in Gerhard Kittel, *Theological Dictionary of the New Testament*, Vol 2, pp. 468f. He gives the other theologically important uses of *ekcheo*, 'pour out,' as the violent killing of martyrs, e.g. Matt.23:25, Acts 22:20, Rev.16:6 and the death of Jesus, Mark 14:24, Matt.26:28, Luke 22:20.
5. Even when not referring explicitly to Pentecost, Paul still uses this metaphor to describe God's love which 'has been poured into our hearts through the Holy Spirit,' Rom.5:5. The close link which he makes between the Holy Spirit and 'pouring out' is also shown in Titus 3:55–6 where he speaks of Christ's 'regeneration and renewal in the Holy Spirit, which he poured out on us.' Cf. Johannes Behm in Gerhard Kittel, *Theological Dictionary of the New Testament*, Vol 2, pp. 468f.
6. For standard works on history and doctrine see Donald Gee, *Wind and Flame, The Pentecostal Movement*, John Thomas Nicol, *The Pentecostals*, Vinson Synam, *The Holiness-Pentecostal Movement in the United States*, Walter J. Hollenweger, *The Pentecostals*.
7. For standard works on history and doctrine see P. E. Shaw, *The Catholic Apostolic Church*, Roland A. Davenport, *Albury Apostles*.
8. Valentine Cunningham, 'Texts and their Stories — 14,' *Redemption Tidings*, October 1970, p. 3: 'And the theological awareness makes Irvingism quite distinct from any isolated but perhaps ill-understood, occurrences of tongues among earlier revivalists; perhaps for the first time since Tertullian the participants knew precisely what was afoot.' Cf. Ronald Knox, *Enthusiasm*, p. 551.
9. For a full account see C. Gordon Strachan, *The Pentecostal Theology of Edward Irving*.
10. Edward Irving, *The Day of Pentecost or the Baptism with the Holy Ghost*.
11. W.H. Hudson, in his Introduction to Thomas Carlyle's, *Sartor Resartus* and *On Heroes and Hero Worship*, p. xii.
12. Thomas Carlyle, *Sartor Resartus*, p. 163.
13. Liz Greene, Relating, *An Astrological Guide to Living with Others on a Small Planet*, p. 266.
14. Liz Greene, *An Astrological Guide to Living with Others on a Small Planet*, p. 267.
15. Thomas Carlyle, *Sartor Resartus*, pp. 127f.
16. *Everyman's Encyclopaedia*, 1950, Vol. 2, p. 68: '*Baphomet*, name of a mysterious idol with 2 heads, male and female, which the Templars were accused of worshipping in secret with licentious rites. The word is a medieval form of Mahomet.'
17. E.g. I. Howard Marshall, *The Gospel of Luke*, p. 146: 'For Luke himself the fulfilment of John's

prophecy was doubtless the event of Pentecost (Acts 1:5) which was also a fulfilment of the prophecy of the outpouring of the Spirit in Joel 2:28; on this view Spirit and fire should not be regarded as alternatives, signifying salvation or judgement.'

18. E.g. G.E.P. Cox, *Saint Matthew*, p. 35; H. Benedict Green, *Matthew*, p. 63; William F. Arndt, *St Luke*, p. 116; W.R.F. Browning, *Saint Luke*, p. 56.

19. Sandra Levy, 'The Importance of Leo in an Aquarian Age,' *The Astrological Journal*, Summer 1984, p. 156.

20. Liz Greene, *An Astrological Guide to Living with Others on a Small Planet*, p. 274.

21. Alan Oken, *Astrology: Evolution and Revolution*, p. 33.

22. For: John L. Sherrill, *They Speak with other Tongues*. Against: John P. Kildahl, *The Psychology of Speaking in Tongues*. Cf. also James D.G. Dunn, *Baptism in the Holy Spirit*.

23. E.g. F.J. Foakes-Jackson, *The Acts of the Apostles,* p. 12: tongues are 'allegorical of the future diffusion of the gospel to all nations.'

24. E.g. F.F. Bruce, *The Acts of the Apostles*, p. 86: 'The reversal of the curse of Babel is surely in the writer's mind.'

25. Vera W. Reid, *Towards Aquarius*, pp. 91f.

26. J.W. Packer, *The Acts of the Apostles*, p. 28.

27. Ernst Haenchen, *The Acts of the Apostles*, p. 169.

28. Ernst Haenchen, *The Acts of the Apostles*, pp. 169–171.

29. Gilles Quispel, *The Secret Book of Revelation*, p. 22.

30. Vera W. Reid, *Towards Aquarius*, p. 92.

31. Alan Oken, *Astrology: Evolution and Revolution*, p. 33.

32. Robert Maddox, *The Purpose of Luke-Acts*, p. 137.

33. Alan Oken, *Astrology: Evolution and Revolution*, p. 31.

34. Alan Oken, *Astrology: Evolution and Revolution*, p. 39.

35. Kenneth G. Cuming, *God and the New Age*, p. 19.

Chapter 9

1. Jean-Jacques Rousseau, *The Social Contract*, Chapter 1, 'Man is born free, and everywhere he is in chains.'

2. Martin Luther King, *Stride Towards Freedom: The Montgomery Story*.

3. William Wilberforce, *Journal*, 28 October, 1787: 'God Almighty has set before me two great objects: the suppression of the slave trade and the reformation of manners.'

4. See Gustave Gutierrex, *A Theology of Liberation*.

5. Alan Oken, *Astrology: Evolution and Revolution*, p. 39.

6. Alan Oken, *Astrology: Evolution and Revolution*, p. 34.

7. C.G. Jung, *Aion*, quoted by Liz Greene, *Relating*, p. 273. Jung is of the opinion that Christ's birth coincided with the great conjunction of Saturn and Jupiter on 29 May, 7 BC, i.e. in Gemini — the Twins: 'One thinks involuntarily of the ancient Egyptian pair of hostile brothers.'

8. Liz Greene, *Relating*, p. 269.

9. Liz Greene, *Relating*, p. 270.

10. Liz Greene, *Relating*, pp. 275f.

11. David Tame, *The Secret Power of Music*, p. 250.

12. Herbert Whone, *The Hidden Face of Music*, p. 57.

13. David Tame, *The Secret Power of Music*, p. 249.

14. Liz Greene, *Relating*, p. 274.

15. George S. Hendry, *Theology of Nature*, p. 78.

16. George S. Hendry, *Theology of Nature*, p. 91: But over all the strife there reigns harmony (*harmonia*, Heraclitus invented the word).'

17. Whether Christ was the incarnation of the specifically Heraclitean definition of the Logos has been the subject of enduring theological debate. Some scholars have maintained that St John was influenced more by late Hellenistic philosophy than by Heraclitus; others that he derived the concept more from the Old Testament doctrine of the Word and Wisdom of God and yet others that he got it from the Gnostics. There are also others who have suggested that certain Greek interpretations of the Logos, such as the Stoic, resembled the Hebrew to such an extent that they may be taken as being practically synonymous. For a comprehensive survey of all shades of opinion, see T.E. Pollard, *Johannine Christology and the Early Church*, pp. 6–15.

18. Justin Martyr, *Apologia* I.46, in Henry Bettenson, Ed. *The Early Christian Fathers*, p. 60.

19. Irenaeus, *Adversus Haereses*, IV 4:2 in Henry Bettenson, *The Early Christian Fathers*, p. 76.

20. Eusebius, *Demonstratio Evangelica*, 4. 13. 2–3, in G.L. Prestige, *God in Patristic Thought*, pp. 35f.

21. See Paul Beasley-Murray, *The Cosmic Christ*, for a very detailed study of Paul's teaching on cosmic Christology.

22. G.L. Prestige, *God in Patristic Thought*, p. 129.

23. T.E. Pollard, *Johannine Christology and the Early Church*, p. 318.

24. Maurice Wiles, *The Christian Fathers*, p. 29.

25. Maurice Wiles, *The Christian Fathers*, p. 31.

26. Liz Greene, *Relating*, pp. 264f.

27. Alfred Douglas, *The Oracle of Change, How to Consult the I Ching*, p. 54. George S. Hendry points out the similarity between Heraclitus and Chinese philosophy of the same period, *Theology of Nature*, p. 153: 'A remarkable parallel to the thought of Heraclitus is to be found in the ancient Chinese doctrine of yang and yin which developed in roughly the same period and in very similar circumstances.'

Chapter 11

1. Carter, Charles E.O. *An Introduction to Political Astrology*, 'Historical Cycles and newly found Planets,' pp. 73–87.

2. Hengel, Martin, *Judaism and Hellenism*, p. 210.

Chapter 12

1. Tarnas, Richard, *Prometheus the Awakener*, pp. 122f.

2. Tarnas, Richard, *Prometheus the Awakener*, pp. 125f.

Bibliography

Adams, Douglas, *The Hitchhiker's Guide to the Galaxy*, Pan, London 1979.

Arndt, William F. *The Gospel According to St Luke*, Concordia, St Louis 1956.

—, *St Luke*, Concordia, St Louis 1956.

Ashe, Geoffrey, *The Ancient Wisdom*, Abacus, London 1977.

Balmforth, H. *The Gospel According to St Luke*, Clarendon, Oxford 1930.

Barclay, William, *The Revelation of St John*, St Andrew Press, Edinburgh 1976.

Bauval, Robert & Adrian Gilbert, *The Orion Mystery*, Heinemann, London 1994.

Beasley-Murray, G.R. *Revelation*, Marshal, Morgan & Scott, London 1974.

Beckwith, Isbon T. *The Apocalypse of John*, Baker Book House, Grand Rapids, 1967.

Bettenson, Henry, ed. *The Early Christian Fathers*, Oxford 1969.

Bonewitz, Ra, *Cosmic Crystals, The hidden world of crystals and the New Age application of crystal energies*, Turnstone, Wellingborough 1984.

Bowker, John, *Jesus and the Pharisees*, Cambridge 1973.

Bragdon, Claude, *The Beautiful Necessity,* Quest Books, London 1978.

Brown, Dan, *The Da Vinci Code*, Doubleday, New York 2003.

Brown, Raymond E. *The Birth of the Messiah*, Chapman, London 1977.

Browning, W.R.F. *The Gospel According to St Luke*, S.C.M., London 1960.

Bruce, F.F. *The Acts of the Apostles*, Tyndale, London 1962.

—, *A New Testament Commentary*, Pickering & Inglis, London & Glasgow 1969.

—, *The Spreading Flame*, Paternoster Press, Exeter 1958.

Bullinger, Ethelbert W. *Number in Scripture*, Eyre & Spottiswoode, London 1894.

Burney, C.F. *The Books of Kings*, Clarendon, Oxford 1937.

Butler, Christopher, *Number Symbolism*, RKP, 1970.

Caird, G.B. *The Revelation of St John the Divine*, Black, London 1966.

Capp, Bernard, *Astrology and the Popular Press*, Faber & Faber, London 1979.

Carlyle, Thomas, *Sartor Resartus* and *On Heroes and Hero Worship*, Everyman's Library, Dent, London 1967.

Carrington, Philip, *The Meaning of the Revelation*, S.P.C.K., London 1931.

Carter, Charles E.O. *An Introduction to Political Astrology*, Fowler, Romford, Essex, 1951.

Cartlidge, David R. & David L. Dungan, in *Documents for the Study of the Gospels*, Collins, London 1980.

Cathie, Captain Bruce, *The Pulse of the Universe: Harmonic 288*, Reed, London 1977.

Charles, R.H. *The Apocrypha and Pseudepigraphia of the Old Testament*, Clarendon, Oxford 1913.

Charles, R.H. *The Book of Jubilees*, Black, London 1902.

—, *The Revelation of St John*, T. & T. Clark, Edinburgh 1920.

Clemen, Carl, *Primitive Christianity and its Non-Jewish Sources*, T. & T. Clark, Edinburgh 1912.

Clifford, Richard J. *The Cosmic Mountain in Canaan and the Old Testament*, Harvard University Press, Cambridge Mass 1972.

Collin, Rodney, *The Theory of Celestial Influence*, Vincent Stuart, London 1954.

Cook, Roger, *The Tree of Life*, Thames & Hudson, Avon, London, New York, 1974

Cooper, J.C. *An Illustrated Encyclopaedia of Traditional Symbols*, Thames & Hudson, London 1978.

Cope, Gilbert, *Symbolism in the Bible and in the Church*, S.C.M., London 1959.

Cox, G.E.P. *Saint Matthew*, S.C.M., London 1958.

Creed, John Martin, *The Gospel According to St Luke*, Macmillan, London 1930.

Cullmann, Oscar, *Christ and Time*, S.C.M., London 1951.

Cuming, Kenneth G. *God and the New Age*, Courier, Tunbridge Wells.

Cunningham, Valentine, *Redemption Tidings*, October 1970.

Cupitt, Don, *The Sea of Faith*, B.B.C., London 1984.

Daniélou, Alain, *Introduction to the Study of Musical Scales*, The India Society, London 1943.

Davenport, Roland A. *Albury Apostles*, United Writers, London 1970.

Doczi, Gyorgy, *The Power of Limits: proportional harmonies in nature, art and architecture*, Shambhala, Boulder, London 1981.

Dodd, C.H. *The Interpretation of the Fourth Gospel*, Cambridge 1953.

Douglas, Alfred, *The Oracle of Change, How to Consult the I Ching*, Penguin, Harmondsworth 1977.

Dunn, James D.G. *Baptism in the Holy Spirit*, S.C.M., London 1970.

Eastern, Burton Scott, *The Gospel According to St Luke*, T. & T. Clark, Edinburgh 1926.

Edersheim, Alfred, *The Temple, Its Ministry and Services*, Eerdmans, Grand Rapids 1978.

Eliot, T.S. *Collected Poems*, Faber & Faber, London 1970 edn.

Ellis, E. Earle, *The Gospel of Luke*, Nelson, London 1966.

Eysenck, H.F. & D.K.B. Nias, *Astrology, Science or Superstition?* Penguin, London 1984.

Farbridge, Maurice, *Studies in Biblical and Semitic Symbolism*, Ktav.Inc., New York 1970.

Farrar, Austin, *A Rebirth of Images*, Dacre, London 1949.

—, *The Revelation of St John the Divine*, Clarendon, Oxford 1964.

Fenton, J.C. *The Gospel of St Matthew*, Pelican, London 1963.

Finegan, Jack, *Handbook of Biblical Chronology*, Princeton 1964.

Foakes-Jackson, F.J. *The Acts of the Apostles*, Hodder & Stoughton, London 1931.

Ford, D.W. Cleverly, *A Reading of St Luke's Gospel*, Hodder & Stoughton, London 1967.

Ford, J. Massyngberde, *Revelation*, Doubleday, New York 1975.

Gärtner, Bertil, *The Areaopagus Speech and Natural Revelation*, Gleerup, Uppsala 1955.

Gauquelin, Michel and Françoise, *The Cosmic Clocks*, Peter Owen, London 1969; *The Truth about Astrology*, Hutchinson, London 1983.

Gee, Donald, *Wind and Flame, The Pentecostal Movement*, Assemblies of God, Croyden 1976.

Geldenhuys, Norval, *Commentary on the Gospel of Luke*, Marshall, Morgan & Scott, London 1950.

Gilbert, Adrian, *Magi, The Quest For a Secret Tradition*, Bloomsbury, London, 1996.

—, *The New Jerusalem*, Corgi Books, London 2003.

—, *Signs in the Sky*, Bantum, London 2000.

Glasson, T.F. *The Revelation of St John*, Cambridge 1969.

Graves, Robert, *The White Goddess*, Faber & Faber, London 1961.

Gray, John, *I and II Kings*, S.C.M., London 1964.

Green, F.W. *The Gospel according to Saint Matthew*, S.C.M., London 1952.

Green, H. Benedict, *Matthew*, Oxford 1975.

Greene, Brian, *The Elegant Universe*, Vintage, London 2000.

Greene, Liz, *Relating, An Astrological Guide to Living with Others on a Small Planet*, Coveture, Whitstable 1984, edn.

Gutierrex, Gustave, *A Theology of Liberation*, S.C.M., London 1983.

Haenchen, Ernst, *The Acts of the Apostles*, Blackwell, Oxford 1971.

Hanson, Ronald H. Preston & Anthony, *The Revelation of St John the Divine*, S.C.M., London 1973.

Hendry, George S. *Theology of Nature*, Westminister, Philadelphia 1980.

Hitching, Francis, *The World Atlas of Mysteries*, Pan, London 1979.

Hollenweger, Walter J. *The Pentecostals*, S.C.M., London 1972.

Hughes, David, *The Star of Bethlehem Mystery*, Corgi, London 1981.

Irving, Edward, *The Day of Pentecost or the Baptism with the Holy Ghost*, Baldwin & Craddock, London 1831.

Jacobson, Thorkild, *Before Philosophy*, Pelican/Penguin 1971.

Jung, C.G. *Aion*, Princeton 1959.

Kee, Howard Clark, *The Origins of Christianity*, S.P.C.K., London 1980.

Keller, Werner, *The Bible as History*, Hodder & Stoughton, London 1967.

Kelper, Thomas, *The Book of Revelation*, Oxford 1957.

Kiddle, Martin, *The Revelation of St John*, Hodder & Stoughton, London 1940.

Kildahl, John P. *The Psychology of Speaking in Tongues*, Hodder & Stoughton, London 1972.

King, Martin Luther, *Stride Towards Freedom: The Montgomery Story*, Harper & Row, New York 1958.

Kittel, Gerhard, ed., *Theological Dictionary of the New Testament*, Eerdmans, Grand Rapids 1964.

Knight, G.A.F. *Leviticus*, St Andrew Press, Edinburgh 1981.

Knox, Ronald, *Enthusiasm*, Oxford 1950.

Ladd, G.E. *A Commentary on the Revelation of John*, Eerdmans 1972.

Lang-Sims, Lois, *The Christian Mystery*, Allen & Unwin, London 1980.

Lawlor, Robert, *Sacred Geometry, Philosophy and Practice*, Thames & Hudson, London 1982.

Lemesurier, Peter, *The Gospel of the Stars*, Compton, Tilsbury 1977.

Leupold, H.C. *Exposition of Genesis,* Evangelical Press, London 1942.

McClain, Ernest, *The Myth of Invariance*, Shambhala, Boulder 1978.

Maddox, Robert, *The Purpose of Luke-Acts*, Vandenhoeck & Ruprecht, Göttingen 1982.

Manson, W. *The Gospel of Luke*, Hodder & Stoughton, London 1930.

Marshall, I. Howard, *The Gospel of Luke*, Paternoster, Exeter 1978.

Meecham, Henry G., *The Oldest Version of the Bible,* Holborn, London 1932.

Metzger, Bruce M. *A Textual Commentary on the Greek New Testament*, United Bible Societies, London 1975.

Michell, John, *City of Revelation*, Abacus, London 1973.

Montgomery, James A. *The Books of Kings*, T. & T. Clark, Edinburgh 1951.

Morris, Leon, *The Revelation of St John*, Tyndale, London 1969.

Moule, C.F.D. *The Origin of Christology*, Cambridge 1977.

Mumford, Lewis, *The City in History*, Secker & Warburg, London 1961.

Murchie, Guy, *Music of the Spheres*, Rider/Hutchinson, London 1961.

Neugebauer, Otto, *The Exact Sciences in Antiquity*, Dover, New York 1969.

Newbolt, M.R. *The Book of Unveiling*, S.P.C.K. London 1952.

Newton, Eric & William Neil, *The Christian Faith in Art*, Hodder & Stoughton, London 1966.

Nicol, John Thomas, *The Pentecostals*, Logos, Planfield 1971.

Nolan, Albert, *Jesus Before Christianity, The Gospel of Liberation*, Darton, Longman & Todd, London 1977.

Norman, Cohn, *The Pursuit of the Millennium*, Temple Smith, London 1970.

Northcott, Michael, *An Angel Directs the Storm*, IB Tauris, London 2004.

Noth, Martin, *Leviticus*, S.C.M. 1965.

Oken, Alan, *Astrology: Evolution and Revolution*, Bantam, New York 1976.

Packer, J.W. *The Acts of the Apostles*, Cambridge 1966.

Pennick, Nigel, *Sacred Geometry*, Turnstone, Wellingborough 1980.

Playfair, Guy Lyon & Scott Hill, *The Cycles of Heaven*, Pan, London 1979.

Plummer, Alfred, *The Gospel According to St Luke*, T. & T. Clark, Edinburgh 1905.

Pollard, T.E. *Johannine Christology and the Early Church*, Cambridge 1970.

Porter, J.R. *Leviticus*, Cambridge 1976.

Prestige, G.L. *God in Patristic Thought*, S.P.C.K., London 1964.

Quispel, Gilles, *The Secret Book of Revelation*, Collins, London 1979.

Rad, Gerhard von, *Genesis,* S.C.M., London 1961.

Reid, Vera W. *Towards Aquarius*, Aquarian, London 1969.

Robinson, J. *The First Book of Kings*, Cambridge 1972.

Robinson, Theodore H. *The Gospel of Matthew*, Hodder & Stoughton, London 1927.

Russell, D.S. *The Jews from Alexander to Herod*, Oxford 1967.

Sagan, Carl, *Cosmos*, Book Club Associates, London 1980.

Santillana, Giorgio de & Hertha von Dechend, *Hamlet's Mill*, Gambit, Ipswich 1969

Schick, Edward, *The Revelation of St John*, Sheed & Ward, London.

Scholes, Percy, *The Concise Oxford Dictionary of Music*, London, Oxford 1973.

—, *The Oxford Companion to Music*, Oxford.

Sendrey, Alfred, *Music in Ancient Israel*, Vision, London 1969.

Seymour, P.A.H. *The Birth of Christ, Exloring the Myth*, London, Virgin, 1998.

Shaffer, E.S., *Kubla Khan and the Fall of Jerusalem*, Cambridge 1975.

Shaw, P.E. *The Catholic Apostolic Church*, King's Crown, New York 1946.

Sherrill, John L. *They Speak with other Tongues*, Hodder & Stoughton, London 1964.

Simcox, W.H. *The Revelation,* Cambridge 1902.

Snaith, N.H. *Leviticus and Numbers,* Nelson, London 1967.

Sorrell, Charles A. & George F. Sandstrom, *The Rocks and Minerals of the World*, Collins, London 1982.

Stirling, William, *The Canon*, Garnstone, London 1974.

Strachan, C. Gordon, *The Pentecostal Theology of Edward Irving, Darton, Longman & Todd,* London 1973.

Swete, Henry, *The Apocalypse of St John*, Macmillan, London 1907.

Synam, Vinson, *The Holiness-Pentecostal Movement in the United States*, Eerdmans, Grand Rapids 1971.

Tame, David, *The Secret Power of Music*, Turnstone, Wellingborough 1984.

Tarnas, Richard, *Prometheus the Awakener*, Spring, Woodstock, Connecticut, 1995.

Temple, Robert, *The Crystal Sun*, Arrrow Books, London, 2000.

—, *The Sirius Mystery*, Sidgwick & Jackson, London 1976.

Thompson, G.H.P., *The Gospel According to Luke*, Oxford 1972.

Tinsley, E.J. *The Gospel According to Luke*, Cambridge 1965.

Uyldert, Mellie, *The Magic of Precious Stones*, Turnstone, Wellingborough 1981.

Varley, Desmond, *Seven: the Number of Creation*, G. Bell, London 1976.

Walvoord, John F. *The Revelation of Jesus Christ*, Marshall, Morgan & Scott, London 1966.

Whone, Herbert, *Church, Monastery, Cathedral, A Guide to the Symbolism of Christian Tradition*, Compton Russell Element 1977.

—, *The Hidden Face of Music*, Gollancz, London 1974.

Wiles, Maurice, *The Christian Fathers*, Hodder & Stoughton, London 1966.

Yardin, L. *The Tree of Light*, Horovitz, London 1971.

Index

Chartres

Sacred Geometry, Sacred Space

Gordon Strachan

Gordon Strachan explores the magnificent structure of Chartres Cathedral, and examines the influences on the medieval master builders.

Using Chartres as a starting point, he suggests that the origins of the Gothic style may lie in Islamic architecture. He goes on to consider how the experience of a particular architectural space affects us, and how sacred geometry works.

Beautifully illustrated in a large format, this is an inspiring and informative book for anyone interested in religious architecture and spirituality.

Floris Books

Jesus the Master Builder

Druid Mysteries and the Dawn of Christianity

Gordon Strachan

The activities of Jesus before the start of his ministry at the age of thirty have been the subject of much speculation. Did he travel beyond the bounds of Palestine in his search for wisdom knowledge? Where did he acquire the great learning which amazed those who heard him preaching and enabled him to cross swords in debate with Scribes and Pharisees?

A number of legends suggest that Jesus travelled to the British Isles with Joseph of Arimathea, who worked in the tin trade. With these legends as his starting point, Gordon Strachan uncovers a fascinating network of connections between the Celtic world and Mediterranean culture and philosophy, from the secret geometry of masons and builders, which Jesus would have encountered in his work as a craftsman in Palestine, to the Gematria or number coding of the Old and New Testaments.

Floris Books